What Experts Are Saying about
Innovative Planning: Your Church in 4-D

"If you want to know best practices for planning in an innovative congregation, you should listen to the words of a successful innovative pastor. Through this book Bud Wrenn, speaking from the platform of success in innovative congregational ministry, provides proven methods for innovative a
for congregations."

George Bullard, The Columbia Par
Every Congregation Needs a Little Con

"Like so many pastors, my training equip
be doctrinally sound, and care for people. The gaping hole
in my own education was organizational leadership. Many
good pastors and good ministries have been torpedoed by
poor process and planning skills. This practical book from Bud
Wrenn can help leaders navigate the choppy waters of change
and innovation. Bud has many years of experience down in the
trenches of local ministry. His planning roadmap will benefit
every leader."

Lance Witt, founder of Replenish Ministries and former
executive pastor at Saddleback Church

"Bud has taken the elements of organizational theory and
skillfully applied them to the church and church leadership.
While the concepts of business and church may sometimes seem
far apart, the 4D process provides good guiding principles for
the 'business of church.'"

Pat Flippin, vice-president and chief operation officer,
Kingsdown Corporation

"With *Innovative Planning: Your Church in 4D*, Bud Wrenn offers
a start-to-finish primer for those ministry leaders whose native
tongue is not strategy. He goes beyond theory to share some
of the nuts and bolts of what has made him an effective pastor,
leader, and colleague. His insights are certain to help others.
Easy to understand, a delight to read, and helpful at every turn,
Innovative Planning is an excellent contribution to the church."

Chad Hall, Coach Approach Ministries, author of *Coaching
for Christian Leaders*

"*Innovative Planning: Your Church in 4-D* is a must read....as it outlines an exciting and innovative approach to developing a strong foundation for any organization. The book focuses on the organization's infrastructure, with methods and a message that are fresh. I look forward to introducing 4-D within our corporate environment."

   Donna Bruno, president, Logistics Corporation

"This is a relevant, practical book with ideas that can be immediately put to use. Great stories illustrate the points, drawing the reader in. I loved it and learned some things, too!"

   Linda J. Miller, The Ken Blanchard Companies

"Many books that I read have a shelf life of about three to five years. They give valuable information and knowledge, only to be replaced by the next book that comes along. *Innovative Planning: Church in 4-D* is a different kind book. A quality leader, Bud provides practical knowledge of principles that transcends every context with dynamics that are timeless. I would encourage you to buy this book and begin living into these principles."

   Rick Hughes, senior consultant for Discipleship for North Carolina Baptists

INNOVATIVE PLANNING

BOOKS BY
The Columbia Partnership Ministry Partners

George W. Bullard Jr.
Every Congregation Needs a Little Conflict
Pursuing the Full Kingdom Potential of Your Congregation

Richard L. Hamm
Recreating the Church

Edward H. Hammett
Reaching People under 40 while Keeping People over 60:
Being Church to All Generations

Spiritual Leadership in a Secular Age:
Building Bridges Instead of Barriers

A full listing and description of TCP resources is available at
www.chalicepress.com and
www.thecolumbiapartnership.org

INNOVATIVE PLANNING

Your Church in 4-D

BUD WRENN

CHALICE
P R E S S

ST. LOUIS, MISSOURI

Cover and interior design: Elizabeth Wright

Visit Chalice Press on the World Wide Web at
www.chalicepress.com

10 9 8 7 6 5 4 3 2 1   08   09   10   11   12   13

Library of Congress Cataloging-in-Publication Data

Wrenn, Bud.
    Innovative planning : your church in 4-D / Bud Wrenn.
        p. cm.
    ISBN 978-0-8272-1650-1
    1. Church management. I. Title.

BV652.W74 2009
254—dc22   2008044132

Printed in United States of America

Contents

Acknowledgments

I always wanted to do this, as I would read other authors thanking folks for their help in enabling them to write their books. So here goes!

To my buddies—Gary, Bob, Richard, and David, my "small group," who have been long-time loyal colleagues in the work of helping pastors develop their leadership skills. Their camaraderie has been life to me over the past eight years.

A big thanks to my staff—past and current—at Integrity, who have helped me learn lessons in leading in a congregational environment. Rick, Steven, Jamie, Cody, Chuck, Donna, Steve, Jon, you all over the years have been—and are—a joy to work with! Thanks for sticking!

To George and Esther and their family, whose hospitality has allowed me to learn firsthand from some of the best teachers about church health and growth.

To Doug and Terry, whose lives of loyalty and faithfulness down through the years have given so many—especially me—a beautiful picture of the heart of Jesus.

To my Mom, the retired English teacher, whose editing skills gave her an outlet to *continue* correcting my grammar, and Dad, both of whom have always believed in me.

Finally, and most importantly, are my wife, Tammy, and three kids—Jacob, Hannah, and Katy, who allowed me to block out time—even their time—to do this writing thing. Not only did they allow me the time. They protected my "writing time"! I love you all so much!

Editor's Foreword

Inspiration and Wisdom for Twenty-First-Century Christian Leaders

You have chosen wisely in deciding to study and learn from a book published in **The Columbia Partnership Leadership Series** with Chalice Press. We publish for

- Congregational leaders who desire to serve with greater faithfulness, effectiveness, and innovation.
- Christian ministers who seek to pursue and sustain excellence in ministry service.
- Members of congregations who desire to reach their full kingdom potential.
- Christian leaders who desire to use a coach approach in their ministry.
- Denominational and parachurch leaders who want to come alongside affiliated congregations in a servant leadership role.
- Consultants and coaches who desire to increase their learning concerning the congregations and Christian leaders they serve.

The Columbia Partnership Leadership Series is an inspiration- and wisdom-sharing vehicle of The Columbia Partnership, a community of Christian leaders who are seeking to transform the capacity of the North American church to pursue and sustain vital Christ-centered ministry. You can connect with us at www.TheColumbiaPartnership. org.

Primarily serving congregations, denominations, educational institutions, leadership development programs, and parachurch organizations, the Partnership also seeks to connect with individuals, businesses, and other organizations seeking a Christ-centered spiritual focus.

We welcome your comments on these books, and we welcome your suggestions for new subject areas and authors we ought to consider.

George W. Bullard Jr., Senior Editor
GBullard@TheColumbiaPartnership.org

The Columbia Partnership,
332 Valley Springs Road, Columbia, SC 29223-6934
Voice: 803.622.0923, www.TheColumbiaPartnership.org

Foreword

Visionary leadership says, "We're going to do it!" As a senior pastor my job is to continually keep the church on track to fulfilling its purpose. That gets harder and harder the larger the church gets. So my number one responsibility is to continually clarify and communicate the vision of Saddleback Church. I'm constantly answering the questions, What are we doing? Why are we here? Where are we going? And we do that through classes, articles, slogans, symbols, in any way we can. It's important to tell people the reason we are here.

Proverbs says, "Without a vision the people perish." So the difference between a dream and a vision is that a vision is a pragmatic dream. Lots of people have great dreams, but they can never get them in a concrete form where you can do something about it. A vision is a dream that can be implemented. It's specific. Nothing becomes dynamic until it becomes specific.

Most churches I've been in have lots of talent, but they don't have a unifying vision to motivate that talent into action. It's wasted talent just sitting on the sidelines, not being used. If you have a vision and it's significant and it's meaningful, you will attract and motivate people.

So you may be asking, "How can we capture, communicate, and infuse the vision into the culture of our church so it influences all we do?"

In his book *Innovative Planning: Your Church in 4-D* Bud Wrenn answers that question. He shows you a systematic approach to planning that ensures all you do lines up with that vision. Any church leaders can influence their church to accomplish that vision by reading this book and applying its principles.

Rick Warren
Senior Pastor, Saddleback Church

Introduction

Equipped with a just-earned permit, I climbed in for my first official ride. Quickly, I discovered that driving a car is not necessarily as easy as it looks. I had been driving for a long time, since about age twelve, on the family farm, and even on the obscure paved state road that connected the farm property to the nearest major highway. So I had some experience. The 1965 "four on the floor" red Ford Mustang coupe was the car that I would drive in a few months when I got my license. It was also the car my dad found most appropriate to drive to the farm, on the farm, and around the farm. In other words, our Mustang—no—*my* Mustang, was really a farm truck disguised as a car—and, for the most part, it *looked* like a farm truck disguised as a car!

One day I suddenly found the Mustang really difficult to steer. I had to exert a good bit of effort just to make the steering wheel move. I felt like I was having a workout every time I drove. I didn't ask Dad about it, thinking that was the way it was supposed to be.

Finally, one day my dad said something like, *"I've really got to get an alignment on this car."* Knowing little about the intricacies of an automobile, I asked him what an alignment was. He explained to me, in an elementary-level lesson, that alignment is what is done to adjust the wheels to bring them in line with the chassis of the car. When the car is in alignment, he told me, it is much easier to steer. Also the tires wear more evenly, and, basically, many of the component parts of the car will last longer. Made sense to me.

I finally understood why the car never really "felt right." I had just thought that's the way it was! After the alignment was done, I thought I was driving a new car—uh, I mean, farm truck!

Many organizations—businesses, congregations, athletic teams, civic clubs, etc.—are like that 1965 Mustang I drove. They are out of alignment and in serious need of adjustment. Many of the leaders in these organizations are like I was—they are leading, or trying to lead, oblivious to the real condition of the organization, just as I was to the condition of the Mustang!

Organizational Alignment

Organizational alignment occurs when the component parts of an organization are pointed in the same direction. What are the

1

component parts? Well, just about everything. The employees, members, associates, and whatever other terms are used to describe the people of the organization and their roles are component parts. The physical assets—equipment, machinery, and facilities—are component parts. Even the intangibles such as philosophy, beliefs, values, and vision are component parts.

Although the word *alignment* may not appear too often in the following pages, this book is really about organizational alignment and how to make it happen in your organizational context. The best way for an organization to have alignment is to intentionally create an overall framework that facilitates and preserves alignment. The organization must plan for it and work the plans that will create and sustain it.

In this book, we will look at some *not so new ideas* in a new way. We will see how organizational planning, with great intentionality, is the primary vehicle for organizational alignment. What I propose is not a *cookie-cutter mold*, or a *one-size-fits-all model* of organizational planning. Rather, I will present a paradigm that will hopefully drive a new perspective about organizational planning. Within the paradigm, an organization develops its own unique process, designed to fit its organizational context.

While we will place more emphasis on planning and execution in a congregational context, these principles will work in any organization—*for profit* and *not for profit*. I quite frequently hear people, particularly church leaders, say something like, *"That may work in the business world, but it won't work in church."* I have a real problem with that position. If a principle works, and is in line with accepted ethical and moral standards, then why can't it work—in any organizational setting? After all, very little separates business principles and church principles. We should think, rather, in terms of *organizational* principles. Because the primary target audience for this book is the innovative congregation and congregations moving toward becoming innovative, most of the examples in this book are set in congregational contexts.

In this book we will advocate a consistent corporate language around planning for the organization. We will identify four key dimensions of planning that should be viewed sequentially and that should facilitate a consistent direction for the organization. To ensure a unified direction, these four dimensions must all be aligned. These four dimensions, when staffed properly to allow organizational members to contribute in the planning process, can *drive significant ownership* among those members. The greater the level of ownership, the greater the organizational alignment and the greater the chance of organizational success.

Finally, we will see that to be healthy, planning must be cyclical. As the organization works through plans, it discovers new things about its environment and its own internal context. It makes adjustments based on these discoveries, and adjusts plans accordingly, on a real-time basis. *Planning, then, in a healthy organization, is a very dynamic process.* Planning becomes nearly as important a pursuit as the actual delivery of the organization's product or service to its customers. The quality of the organization's planning, then, becomes the main determinant of the organization's long-term effectiveness.

Where Is God in Planning?

When I discuss things such as planning with congregations, I invariably encounter the person who asks a question like, "*Where does the Holy Spirit fit into your process?*" or, "*Shouldn't we wait on God to show us what to do in His timing?*" While I understand and respect the thinking that leads to these questions, I feel I must lay out some underlying foundational assumptions concerning the contents of this book. I like to refer to these as "givens." In other words, for planning to be successful, it's a "given" that these things are already done or are being worked on.

1. Prayerful Preparation. All planning concerning the Kingdom of God must be approached with great prayer and prayerful attitudes. In writing this, I am assuming that *it is a given that a congregation is willing to spend time in prayer* and is seeking God's wisdom prior to beginning a planning process and during the process. This book doesn't address such techniques and approaches for doing that. There are, however, many others that do.

2. God Blesses Planning. The Bible is not "anti-planning." Rather, the book of Proverbs *advocates planning, and gives strong advice on how planning can be done effectively.* Here are just a few of those verses that give such good directions on the subject of planning.

> Commit your actions to the Lord,
>   and then your plans will succeed. (Prov. 16:3)

> We can make our plans,
>   but the Lord determines our steps. (Prov. 16:9)

> You can make many plans,
>   but the Lord's purpose will prevail. (Prov. 19:21)

Plans succeed through good counsel;
   don't go to war without wise advice. (Prov. 20:18)

Good planning and hard work lead to prosperity,
   but hasty shortcuts lead to poverty. (Prov. 21:5)

3. Wisdom from God. I'm one of those who believes that often the statement, *"Let me pray about it,"* can be, in many ways, a cop-out. Don't get me wrong—I used the operative words *often, can be,* and *in many ways* to qualify that statement. We all have decisions on which we may be afraid to pull the trigger. In many of these cases, we truly want to hear from God. Often we unnecessarily delay those decisions, waiting to hear from God, when He has already given us the wisdom to figure it out. We miss windows of opportunity. We tend to forget that in addition to working through the nudging of the Holy Spirit, God also works through His equipping us with His wisdom. James 1:5–6 speaks to this fantastic provision that God gives in response to our request! "If any of you lacks wisdom, he should ask God, who gives generously to all without finding fault, and it will be given to him. But when he asks, he must believe and not doubt, because he who doubts is like a wave of the sea, blown and tossed by the wind" (NIV).

So, perhaps the best preparation for planning may be the *daily habit of praying for God's wisdom.* After all, He gave us all brains to use in making decisions, and He offers the wisdom that is needed to *fuel these brains.* We need to ask for it, use it, and trust it.

Alignment and Planning

In summary, effective organizational planning facilitates alignment in an organization, and organizational alignment enables effective planning. The two are simply inseparable. So, let's take a hard look at effective organizational planning!

PART I

A Flexible Process for Innovative Churches

The planning paradigm presented in this book is not a model. It is more of *a flexible and "customizable" approach that any organization can use.* We will refer to it periodically as "4D," in recognition of the four dimensions of planning so foundational to the paradigm. In a congregational context, *4D* can be used to implement nearly any established type of methodology. For example, since its inception twelve years ago, my home church has always been based on the "Purpose Driven" model. A real breakthrough came for us when our context was well enough defined that we could customize, or contextualize, the Purpose Driven model to match who we had become. After all, that's exactly what Rick Warren and other proponents of "PD" encourage: *"Take the PD philosophy and methodology and make it your own."*

Because it is a flexible, customizable framework, the 4D paradigm will work if a church wants to implement the *Purpose Driven model,* the *Connecting Church model* from Pantego Church in Ft. Worth, the *Foyer/Kitchen/Living Room model* from North Pointe Church in Atlanta, a *Willow Creek model,* or just about any other model.

Too many congregations don't understand the value of quality planning or the relationship between the quality of the plans and the success of the congregation. The purpose of a good solid plan is to provide an ultimate destination for the congregation, the direction it must take to move toward that destination, and the detailed steps required to maintain that direction. The 4D Planning Paradigm provides a way for congregations to achieve that purpose.

1

Why Is Planning So Misunderstood?

Jason Conner loved this wave his church was riding. Two years ago he had come to serve as pastor of Creekside Community Church. Creekside was a five-year-old congregation—one that had started as a mission church of Grace Baptist Church, a solid sixty-year-old congregation that, over the years, had had significant impact in its small town.

The Beginning: The Grace Model

Grace had realized a few years ago that it had been successful as a church because of its tendency to look beyond its own congregation. The church had started numerous ministries geared toward impacting those in the community. Their approach was to evangelize through service. Some ministries that proved successful, such as the *Great Shepherd Food Distribution Center*, were "spun off" to become independent agencies. Many ministries had successful runs, but eventually lost their effectiveness and were shut down. The church still maintained a few other ministries.

During recent years, the neighborhood in which Grace is located had begun to change significantly. A largely Caucasian middle-class demographic gradually gave way to a more middle- to lower–middle-class demographic much more diverse in terms of ethnicity. As a result, Grace had found the neighborhood to be much less responsive to their ministry offerings.

As it became apparent to the Grace leadership that this demographic shift would continue, the congregation began to explore new ways to reach the community. They chose to invest in a ministry a young adult Sunday School class suggested six years earlier—sponsor a mission church across town. The easy interstate freeway access in that area had attracted new businesses—both service-oriented and retail. In addition, real estate developers had begun to redefine the area as a bedroom community for the large town twenty-five miles up the interstate, resulting in a few new *suburban* housing developments.

Realizing that this new church could be a good way to retain some Grace members who didn't feel they could identify with the changing community and to reach new folks in a different area of town, the Grace leadership team cautiously accepted the idea. A year later, fourteen of the thirty-two members of the class left Grace to launch Creekside Community Church. This *core group* recruited a recent seminary graduate, a nephew of one of its members, to serve as its pastor. The new congregation rented the auditorium of one of the two elementary schools in town and began meeting.

The Creekside Experiment

The first two years of Creekside's ministry were extremely difficult. About fifty people came when the church opened. However, they found little opportunity to get connected beyond the Sunday morning experience. The core group had committed to emphasize *small groups,* but the immediate needs of keeping the fledgling church going seemed to divert the leaders' focus from a number of important things, such as small groups. They did not create a Sunday School.

The founding team had obviously underestimated the complexity of launching a new church. The inexperience of the young pastor had proven to be a significant hindrance in getting the new church to solid footing. Just after the congregation's two-year anniversary, the young pastor realized he was in over his head and left for a youth pastor position in an established church in a neighboring town. Six of the fourteen core team members left the church at the time of the pastor's departure. Attendance, which had never really taken off, dropped to an average of forty, down almost half from its average in the first two years. The other eight core members had committed with each other to try it once again.

After a year of prayer and developing a picture of what they really wanted Creekside to be, the remaining core group members set out to find a pastor who could lead them toward that picture.

A six-month search led them to a pastor at a small, but growing, traditional church, Antioch Church, in a neighboring state.

Rebooting Creekside Church

Jason Connor had taken the pastorate of Antioch, his first, three years prior. He had gone back to seminary after an eight-year stint as a fireman. Jason's dynamic personality and "down to earth" persona had captured the hearts of folks in this small town. When Jason began his ministry at the church, many came out of simple curiosity, liked what they saw, and stayed.

These same qualities—plus Jason's track record at Antioch—attracted the Creekside team to Jason. In his three years, attendance had increased by 125 percent. The number of baptisms at Antioch, a key metric in the denomination, had increased by a factor of twelve over that of the year prior to Jason's arrival. Amazingly, the average age of the congregation had moved from sixty to forty-two.

While seeing real success in his first pastorate, Jason had gotten caught up in what he was hearing about the more "contemporary" churches, which utilized a different kind of methodology to reach people who were not *churched*. He liked the ideas of a more casual atmosphere, music that was more upbeat and in tune with what folks were listening to on the radio, and the use of multimedia in the context of the worship service. These ideas caused a little unsettledness in Jason's mind. He was intrigued. What if God's plan for him really was to pastor a church that looked like that? These thoughts dominated Jason's mind over the next few months. He often thought about what Antioch could be if Sunday mornings looked like that! He came to the conclusion that the folks at Antioch would likely never embrace such changes, and even if they did, Jason didn't have confidence that he would know what to do to make it happen.

Then came the phone call.

The Creekside Call

The call was from the pastoral search team of a struggling fifty-member congregation called Creekside Community Church. The church wanted to be a major factor in its community and wanted to use contemporary methods to reach those who weren't in church in their area. To Jason, the search team seemed to be a group of honest, authentic folks. He almost immediately sensed a good fit with them.

The three-month "courtship" between Creekside and Jason comprised lots of phone conversations and prayer. Each side agreed to proceed cautiously, not wanting to rush anything. Gradually, everyone seemed to feel progressively better about the potential in the relationship. About one hundred days after their first phone conversation, Jason accepted the offer to become the new pastor at Creekside, despite the significant pay cut he would have to take. He saw great opportunity and, most importantly, God's hand all over this move.

However, two years into his leadership at Creekside, Jason faced a real challenge. He had focused primarily on transforming a dull Sunday service into a vibrant worship experience. Attendance increased steadily until Creekside had to go to two services in the rented high school facilities. A number of the new arrivals were excellent musicians, and some would ultimately form a dynamic worship band. The church's music had become the calling card for CCC.

The Creekside Crossroad

But Jason found himself at a crossroad. For the most part, the 250-plus people at CCC enjoyed being there. Excitement was high. But a number of the regulars at Creekside began asking Jason, *"What's next for Creekside?"* They, like so many, loved the energetic services at CCC. But many of them realized that church goes far beyond Sunday morning. To them, a number of areas needed further development.

The leadership team, consisting of Jason and the other eight core team members, realized that not a lot seemed to be getting accomplished in the church. Volunteer commitment was fairly tenuous and sporadic. The children's ministry was quite large with all the young families that had begun attending Creekside, requiring a large volunteer crew. Nearly as much time was spent finding substitutes for regular Sunday morning workers, as was spent in recruiting regular workers in the first place. Also, sustaining a small groups ministry was very difficult, as it seemed that Creekside people just didn't seem to *do church stuff* once Sunday morning was over.

As this question of *"What's next?"* became more prominent, Jason got a little queasy. He really didn't know what was next for Creekside. He knew that discovering the answer would involve some significant planning time. Being a spontaneous kind of guy, planning was something he didn't think came naturally to him. After all, in Antioch, his first church, the rural congregation was basically run by the deacon board. Jason's most significant planning had to do with what to teach on Sundays. He generally took direction from the deacons.

Feeling a little lost as to what to do next, Jason decided to do what a pastor friend of his did—he would take the CCC Leadership Team on a weekend planning retreat. Maybe "the team" could figure out what was next. But this brought up the next dilemma for Jason—what would they do on the retreat? How would they go about answering the *"What's next?"* question?

Jason had attended many church growth & health conferences. In these conferences, he had sat under the teaching of some of the most celebrated leaders in the Christian world. He also had read some of the top books that addressed the same things. Therefore, Jason felt that he had a pretty good idea of how a healthy, growing congregation should look. Just as he had visualized what Antioch would look like with a more contemporary style of worship and atmosphere, he had done the same with Creekside. Only with Creekside, he had focused his imagination on more than just what could be seen on the surface on Sunday mornings. With Creekside, he thought about the *underlying, foundational principles* that would help the congregation reach a level of health.

Before he had come to Creekside, the congregation had developed a fairly clear picture of how the church should look in the future. Jason had bought into that picture and added some thoughts and ideas that the Creekside folks embraced—even before he agreed to come aboard as the pastor of Creekside.

Creekside's Confusion: Pastoring ≠ Leading

But Jason's struggle had always been, and continued to be, with the question *"How do we get there?"* In the conferences he had attended, and in the books he had read, Jason never felt he had discovered the answer to that question. Now, just a week before the retreat, twenty-seven Creekside members had committed to participate. He knew the right questions were *"Where do we go?"* and *"How do we get there?"* But he had no answer. What would he do with them? What would the retreat look like? What would they get accomplished? Now that queasy feeling felt like a chronic condition.

Jason's problem was not the conferences he was attending or the books he was reading. He was an eager learner. The conferences and books helped him develop a personal picture of *what could be* for his ministry and the congregations he served. The real issue was the fact that in the conferences and books, he didn't think he had run across anything that looked like it would help his congregation get from here to there. He simply hadn't seen what he considered a user-friendly planning process—one that would work for a novice like himself.

Jason is like so many other pastors who are faced with the big task of leading a church. Pastoring and leading can require totally different skill sets. Planning and carrying out church activities, sermon series, and pastoral care duties are quite different from leading people to plan together for the future of a church, and different from leading people in carrying out those plans.

■ **Pastoring and leading can require totally different skill sets.**

To make things even more confusing, transferring the information gleaned from conferences and books, while usually quite valuable, into the local church context is often difficult. Jason's—and Creekside's—situation highlights some typical problems with planning in the church.

Problems in Planning: Inadequate Approaches

Many churches believe themselves to be effective at planning. But all too many do not realize they are taking faulty approaches. So, often this results in plateaued churches without a vision of the future.

The Maintenance *Approach*

■ **In many churches, the underlying perception is that there is no need for real planning, as the preservation of the status quo is a high value.**

For many congregations, the standard mode of operation is maintaining the status quo. The congregation simply perpetuates its existence. The focus is most likely on how things have been done in the past. *Doing* church as it has always been done, rather than *being* the church that is relevant in today's world, is most likely the pursuit of this congregation. The desire to operate as it always has offers little or no incentive for innovation. Quickly outdated, these congregations are almost always on the decline. They are dying and are most often unaware of their condition. Seeing no need for significant change, these churches cultivate the underlying perception that they have no need for real planning, as the preservation of the status quo is a high value.

The Big Blob *Approach*

To be successful, a congregation must first recognize the purpose of planning. Jesus spoke of the role of planning in Luke 14:28–29:

> "But don't begin until you count the cost. For who would begin construction of a building without first calculating the cost to see if there is enough money to finish it? Otherwise, you might complete only the foundation before running out of money, and then everyone would laugh at you."

■ **Failure to distinguish the dimensions of planning will ultimately lead to ineffective and unrealistic plans.**

A congregation must recognize the *different dimensions of planning* that must be approached sequentially. For example, effective planning must begin with the big picture and move toward more concrete plans regarding what must be done to bring that big picture to reality. Unfortunately, even the vast majority of well-meaning congregations that do place value in the planning process don't distinguish the different dimensions. They often see planning as one "big blob" and not as a process with unique dimensions. Failure to distinguish these dimensions of planning will ultimately lead to ineffective and unrealistic plans. The reality of these dimensions and how they interrelate is the primary subject we will deal with in the subsequent pages.

The Once and for All *Approach*

Many congregations view planning as a discrete exercise and not as a continuous, systematic process. Because churches are largely volunteer organizations, the task of pulling together a planning effort is often a huge endeavor. For example, a congregation schedules planning meetings, retreats, etc., over a predetermined period of time. Their desire may truly be to develop a solid plan for the congregation. The big challenges are (a) *scheduling the best time* for participants to come together, and (b) once they're available, *getting volunteers to set aside enough time* to make the planning exercise worthwhile. For many churches, just pulling off the planning exercise takes an incredible amount of time and energy. The result may be that these planning efforts, because of those time and energy requirements, become *discrete exercises*. The planning process comes to be viewed in terms of one-time, stand-alone events, which become few and far between.

Two dangers here are quite obvious. First, the plans resulting from the exercise will be shaped and constrained by (a) time limitations and (b) the perspectives of the people available to participate. The planning process in any organization will always be driven by the particulars of the people who participate. The more effective the group of participants, the higher the quality of the ensuing plans.

■   **Effective planning requires a continuous, systematic approach, rather than one that views planning in terms of discrete exercises.**

Second, the congregations' own internal demographics and environmental conditions will inevitably change—perhaps quite rapidly. The congregation embracing discrete planning exercises will then, at some point, find itself working from a *stand-alone* plan developed with assumptions that are no longer valid. This situation will cause such a church to have to wait until the next planning initiative is scheduled before it can address the changing demographic and environmental conditions.

Congregations must be flexible enough to adapt to rapid changes in their environments—both internally and externally. They need to understand that effective planning requires a continuous, systematic approach, rather than one that views planning in terms of discrete exercises.

The Mix and Match *Approach*

I usually kick off planning seminars by asking the groups a question such as, "What words come to your mind when I say the word *planning*? The floodgates usually open. I hear responses— "goals...strategy...timeline...mission statement...action plan... objectives...vision...to-do lists...results..." The list goes on.

Then I'll ask, "Now if all of you in this room were to give me your definitions of each of those words and phrases, how many different sets of definitions would we have?" Then they get the picture. The collective response is usually something along the lines of, "We would have as many different sets of definitions as we have people in the room." That's the point—planning, and planning terms, mean different things to different people.

This is especially significant in congregations where most of the members spend as much as half of their waking time working professionally in noncongregational organizations—nearly all of which have differing ideas of what planning is all about. Their perceptions about planning, then, are most naturally shaped by those organizations in which they spend so much of their time.

So, in congregations, not only do most of the members bring to the table preconceived notions about planning, but they also bring a significant diversity of views of planning, uniquely shaped by the workplace.

A consistent corporate language is a clear prerequisite for effective planning to take place in any organization. Definitions of planning and planning levels often overlap, leading to great confusion. Congregations, then, must *work doubly hard to bring clarity to their corporate language* with regard to planning simply because of the diversity of views among their people. Although this will take great amounts of time and attention to detail, the value of *everyone singing from the same sheet of music* is critical in ensuring an effective outcome.

■ **Congregations, then, must work doubly hard to bring clarity to their corporate language with regard to planning.**

The Open Invitation *Approach*

Even with an understanding of the distinct dimensions of planning, congregations may expect leaders to function effectively in planning, with little or no regard to how they are wired and gifted. Even congregations that desire to be innovative can quickly lose their edge if they don't have a proper perspective on using the right people, in the right roles, in the right dimensions, in congregational planning.

Jim Collins speaks of companies who have been able to move from being very good organizations to really great organizations. His research discovered that a key factor is the organization's ability, first, to get the right people into the company ("*...the right person on the right bus...*"), and second, to get the right person into the right position ("*...the right person in the right seat on the bus...*").[1] This is certainly a major key in congregations as well.

Often churches try an *open invitation approach* based on the valid assumption that participation *drives ownership* into people. They want to involve as many people as possible in the planning

---

[1] Jim Collins, *Good to Great* (New York: HarperCollins, 2001), 41.

process. Another less-healthy driver for this approach may be the potential fear of what folks may say if they are left out, or "not invited." Another driver may just be to get enough people together to reach what may be considered *critical mass*—i.e., a certain number of people needed to be involved to validate the process.

The danger of the *open invitation* is the possibility of having people involved in types of planning that they are not comfortable with, or equipped to, participate in. This can lead to ineffectiveness in the process and a faulty final product.

■ **The danger of the open invitation is the possibility of having people involved in types of planning that they are not comfortable with, or equipped to participate in.**

If an organization understands that planning has distinct dimensions, then it has to accept two related realities. First, *not everyone is geared toward working in all the dimensions of planning.* Second, *participants should be focused toward working in the dimension(s) of planning in which they are truly comfortable.*

Faulty Perceptions Lead to Faulty Results

With so many churches in the American culture in serious decline or having reached plateaued positions (estimates range anywhere from 60–90 percent), serious consideration has to be given to discovering why this has happened. While surely the factors are far too numerous to be incorporated into this work, we can safely assume that in perhaps the majority of churches the lack of a healthy planning process is a significant contributor. Even in the more innovative churches that I relate to, leaders admit serious deficiencies in their planning processes.

It doesn't make much sense to try to play a game of darts without a dartboard. Darts themselves can be quite dangerous, and if aimed and thrown at the wrong targets, they can cause much damage. Many congregations are doing the same thing. They are playing the "game" of church. Without a planning process that gives them the proper direction, they are like the dart thrower who aims, but has no target. Even if the thrower hits where he aims, he will never know whether his target was the right one. He never knows whether he has won the game.

Pulling It Together

Congregations typically don't utilize healthy planning processes as tools to help them be successful. Perhaps the typical congregation doesn't see the value of healthy planning. Or perhaps the constraints associated with a primarily volunteer organization preclude the typical congregation from being able to invest the time, energy, and resources required to build a healthy planning process. Congregations may be affected by one or more of a number of misconceptions.

- Many congregations are perfectly content to maintain who they have been and what they have. Planning is not necessary as they *see no need for change.*
- Congregations fail to distinguish the *unique dimensions of planning.* They fail to first establish the big picture and then move toward the steps required to make the big picture come to reality.
- Planning in many churches is not viewed as a *continuous, systematic process*, but rather as a discrete, stand-alone event. This leads to a significant inability to adapt to changing demographic and environmental conditions facing the church.
- Few churches have a sense of a *corporate language* with regard to planning. Different terms mean different things to different people. It takes great time and effort to create such a corporate language, as the church has to assimilate the various meanings that members bring into the congregational structure.
- Congregations often expect members to participate in planning, however it may look, with little or no regard to how they are wired and gifted. Planning is a multidimensional process, and people are not typically geared to work effectively in each of these dimensions.

If a church is to be successful, it must embrace the value of planning, and understand some very foundational principles about how planning can be integrated into the life of the congregation.

2

What Does an Innovative Congregation Look Like?

Jason Conner was excited about working with Creekside. His ideas about working in a "contemporary church" such as Creekside were shaped largely by the conferences he'd attended and books he'd read. He obviously had no prior experience in such a church, and when he had come to Antioch he found no churches like CCC around. Taking the pastorate at Creekside, then, had been his first real exposure to the contemporary church. With the pressures of this moment, however, the excitement of those days starting out at Creekside, just a couple of years ago, seemed to be in the distant past.

The Pressure of Planning

As Jason thought about the upcoming planning retreat, he got more and more nervous. He still didn't have much of an idea of how to lead the people who were committed to the retreat, and that was eating away at him. The event was now only seven days away, and he had no idea about the agenda, how to kick it off, how it should wrap up, or even what a successful retreat might look like.

He had been feeling the pressures of those folks asking "*What's next?*" and "*How do we get there?*" Coupled with his drawing a blank about what to do on the retreat, he really began to wonder if he was the guy who could lead Creekside to answer those questions. His nervousness led to doubts about his abilities, and even about his calling to be a pastor.

When he was at Antioch, the congregation's expectations of Jason had been primarily to keep the ball rolling—to teach, visit folks, and to make sure that the ministries, particularly Sunday School, were successfully carried out. The church did not face many big decisions. Any truly big decisions went to the deacon board. They would ask Jason for his opinion, but, by and large, he was not held responsible for those decisions. Even those big decisions at Antioch focused mainly on facilities, budgets, and who would fill which committee positions. Such decisions seemed simplistic in relation to the decisions—directional decisions—that Creekside needed to make.

When Jason left Antioch for Creekside, he looked forward to working in a similar way with the CCC leadership team. He was comfortable that the group that had "courted" him as their pastor had some capable people. They seemed to be fairly well-educated, and, from his questioning of them, a number of them held very responsible vocational positions. But at this point, he wanted to question, *"Where are they now? Why do I have to pull this retreat together—all by myself?"* He needed their help!

"Was it really supposed to be this way?" Jason asked himself. After all, weren't things supposed to run smoother in a *contemporary church*?

Definitions May Define Success

The language game plays an essential role in planning. All participants must understand precisely what each person in the planning process is saying and is meaning. Too often planning teams come together with decidedly different planning vocabularies. So a look at language and language confusion is essential in the planning process.

Label Confusion

Some of the biggest misconceptions in the American church today come as the result of labeling of individual churches. Churches have always been labeled. But those labels primarily have been associated with denominationalism. The *church growth movement* of the past thirty or so years has led to a broader variety of labels, often associated with worship style. In turn, worship style has come to be equated with musical style.

For example, words such as *contemporary* and *innovative* are used to distinguish a church from one that is *traditional*. The term *traditional* has come to represent the "benchmark" to determine how *contemporary* or *innovative* a church really is. *Traditional* typically characterizes a church that uses hymns, and perhaps instruments such as piano and organ. Any musical style that is characterized by more modern praise choruses (even those that may embody 1970s style popular music styles), as well as any other style that is truly indigenous to a church's culture, or uses any other instruments than piano or organ, can always find someone who will label it *contemporary*.

■ **The term *traditional* has come to represent the "benchmark" to determine how contemporary or innovative a church really is.**

Labeling in the church is very subjective. The label is defined in the mind of the individual and shaped by the preferences, tastes, and experiences of the individual. One person's *traditional* church is another's *blended* church. One's *contemporary* church is someone else's *cheesy* church. One's *contemporary* church is someone else's *traditional* church.

Even in the organization that I lead, the Innovative Church Community, with hundreds of participants, inconsistency of labeling causes great confusion. We have purposely moved away from even inquiring about types of churches, simply because of the diversity of labels and the meanings behind them. Many see our name, which includes the word *Innovative*, and assume that participation is only for churches that use upbeat music, or alternative postmodern worship practices.

Defining Contemporary

This confusion of labeling has led to a couple of words coming to be used almost interchangeably. Those words are *contemporary* and *innovative*. But these words are simply not the same! In the purest sense, the word *contemporary*, according to the *American Heritage Dictionary,* has this meaning: "Belonging to the same period of time: a fact documented by two contemporary sources. Of about the same age. Current; modern: contemporary trends in design."

Despite this dictionary definition, we use *contemporary* to describe worship styles that incorporate music and other elements that *don't* 'belong to the same period of time.' In the church labeling business, the word *contemporary* has become a relative term. It is most often used simply to refer to any church characterized by a style that is *not traditional*.

The true idea of being *contemporary* is like shooting at a moving target. Anything that is truly contemporary must be in a nearly constant state of continuous change to keep pace with a changing environment. In that regard, few churches can be truly *contemporary* in the purest sense.

Defining Innovation

The other word in that interchangeable pair, *innovative,* has a totally different meaning than *contemporary.* Again, according to the *American Heritage Dictionary, innovation* refers to "The act of introducing something new. Something newly introduced."

Being innovative, then, has more to do with operating in a mode in which new things are being introduced. An innovative organization, then, might be known as one that...

a. is willing to try new things.
b. encourages its people to come up with new ideas and put them into place.
c. allows experimentation, and
d. doesn't get overly concerned with "failure."

The innovative organization will try things. It successfully redefines "failure" and sees in it the opportunity to learn new things that will enhance chances for success in the future.

> ■ **The innovative organization will try things. It successfully redefines "failure" and sees in it the opportunity to learn new things that will enhance chances for success.**

An innovative congregation, then, is a congregation that is willing to do new things, regardless of whether they may look contemporary, traditional, modern, postmodern, etc. The innovative congregation is one that will do new things because that is the right thing to do. It innovates with purpose and intentionality, not just doing something new for the sake of doing something new. Rather, *it has in mind a larger picture,* one that innovation will help the congregation move toward. The *truly innovative congregation will know...*

a. *when* something new is needed
b. how to figure out *what* is needed
c. what *purpose* the innovation will serve, and
d. what *success* with the innovation will look like.

So—what is innovation? Innovation in a congregation is not defined by style of music, the accepted attire for those who attend worship services, or the use of drama, multimedia, etc., in the services.

Rather, an innovative approach to ministry has *more to do with the way decisions are made and executed*. For example, the innovative congregation will be characterized by a culture that emphasizes (1) staying in touch with *external and internal environmental factors*, and (2) decision processes that are *proactive* and allow for *timely and effective response* to changes in those environmental factors.

The Elements of Innovation

A congregation must key on a number of things if it is to be truly innovative.

First, they must cultivate an *awareness of what is going on inside the church*. This is much easier said than done. The leadership of the typical congregation has very little firsthand exposure to what is really going on in the lives of its members. Members may spend as little as one hour to one-and-a-half hours per week with the rest of the congregation. With this relatively small amount of direct contact time, it is difficult to know what is really going on. It is so easy for leaders to misread the state of the congregation, as their assessments are most likely based on what they observe during these times of direct contact.

Second, church leadership needs a *keen awareness of what is going on in and around the community, region, state*, etc., in which the church is located. These external factors will invariably affect the congregation as a whole, just as they affect the members as individuals. So often, slight shifts in external factors, which have relatively small impact on individual members, can have much more pronounced collective effects on whole congregations. The effects of these shifts are often underestimated and even go undetected.

The third critical element in an innovative approach has to do with the *responsiveness of the congregation with regard to these internal and external factors*. While awareness of these factors is a must, it is not nearly enough. The congregation must have the ability to read and assess the impact of shifts and to act accordingly. In other words, *the congregation's decision-making process must be nimble.*

■ **The congregation's decision-making process must be nimble.**

A truly innovative congregation is one that embodies these three qualities. At the other end of the spectrum is the bureaucratic congregation. The purely bureaucratic congregation is one that is much less likely to take into account the state of its people and internal and external environmental factors. The bureaucracy is much more likely to operate in the manner it has always done. Procedures have been deeply engrained in the organizational structure, and they seldom change. Often, it appears the organization exists for the purpose of self-perpetuation, rather than for the benefit of any customer or client base. As long as the typical bureaucracy can function and perform *well enough,* it will continue in that mode.

Congregations are just as susceptible to becoming bureaucratic as any company—perhaps more so.

■ **Congregations are just as susceptible to becoming bureaucratic as any company—perhaps more so.**

Boats, Bureaucracy, and Innovation

While I am certainly not an expert, I truly adore boating. I love taking my 17″ Bayliner out into the ocean and along the intercoastal waterway. A boating experience a couple of summers ago gives a good picture of the contrast between an innovative organization and a bureaucratic organization. My wife and I, along with another couple, were in some fairly choppy surf near the intersection of the ocean, the intercoastal waterway, and the mouth of the Cape Fear River. As my wife, who is the more cautious one in our relationship, and her friend were talking in the back of the boat, preoccupied in comparing notes about kids and teenagers, I saw in the distance a large freighter, heading down the river and ultimately out to sea. As I noticed that the ladies were engrossed in conversation, I decided to head out toward even choppier waters to ride along with the freighter.

As I increased speed to catch up to the freighter, the bumps from the higher waves caught my wife's attention. As she "gently admonished" me to turn the boat around, I slowed the speed a bit and assured her that we were totally fine. As I neared the freighter, I noticed a few things. First, this freighter was a monster. The closer I got to it, the more imposing it looked! It was really impressive. Second, the exhaust from the engine made it nearly impossible to ride behind the freighter—a bummer since the water in the wake of the freighter was as smooth as glass compared to the rest of the river. Third, I noticed the proximity of the freighter's path in relation to the channel markers, and saw that it had to stay on a fairly narrow path to minimize the risk of running aground. Fourth, I couldn't see anyone on the deck of the freighter. As large as this ship was, I was amazed that there seemed to be no visible person in control! It seemed to be driving itself!

Fifth, I noticed that my small boat could handily navigate the waters around the freighter. I could even pass it, circle it, and come right alongside it. I could make all kinds of maneuvers (at least to the extent that my wife would allow me), and yet the freighter couldn't do these things.

As I thought about that experience much later, I noticed some points of comparison between the freighter and my boat, and organizations.

Bureaucracy and Comfort Zones

That freighter is not unlike the bureaucratic organization—for a number of reasons.

The smoother water in the wake of the freighter's path was really where I wanted to keep my little boat. After all, my wife was right—the water was pretty rough that day. So, as a smaller boat can be quite comfortable riding in the wake of the freighter, a church can be pretty comfortable as a part of a bureaucracy.

■ **The bureaucracy, for all its lack of flexibility, can provide a great ride for those who desire to work or live in a mode that will require little disturbance.**

The bureaucracy, for all its lack of flexibility, can provide a great ride for those who desire to work or live in a mode that will require little disturbance. Many who just want to get by, and who don't care about excellence, can find a home in a bureaucratic organization. They are not likely to get pushed to perform at a level that would challenge the status quo of the organization, or that would challenge their own level of comfort.

Bureaucracy and (the Lack of) Influence

One who chooses to be a part of a bureaucracy will have to put up with some unpleasant stuff. For example, I wanted to follow close behind the freighter that day, but I could only get so close. The exhaust from the freighter could have asphyxiated my passengers and me.

In no way could I influence anything that freighter did that day. Even if I had pulled directly in front of that boat and stopped on a dime, the captain probably would never have been able to stop the freighter before it plowed into my little boat.

This illustrates another aspect of the bureaucracy: It is very difficult for any one person, or group, to have significant influence on the direction or operation of the organization. This can be frustrating for people who are change agents, who want to see their organizations operate more efficiently, and who may desire to have a part in productive change for the sake of their own self-satisfaction.

Bureaucracy and Imagination

As small as my little boat is, I had a couple of advantages over the freighter. I was able to cut this way and that through the surf, but the freighter certainly couldn't. I could ride over toward the shoreline and say "hi" to the fishermen and swimmers and have a good time doing it. But the freighter couldn't. I thought it had to be kind of boring for the captain to just push the ship forward, having to stay right in its narrow, predetermined path.

Again, the bureaucracy is somewhat like this. It has a job to accomplish and is often very rigid in the way it goes about its business. The bureaucracy often leaves little if any room for creativity or for people to use their imaginations. Forces somewhere in the ivory towers of the organization usually predetermine the course. As a result, these organizations will most likely stifle the creativity of their people, leading to one of two outcomes. First, many employees will accept the stifling culture and conform, as a bureaucratic organization can be very comfortable. Second, many will leave the organization—simply because they value their exercise of creativity more than they value the comfort the organization affords. In either case, the organization loses.

■ **There's often not a lot of room for creativity, or for someone to use their imagination, in the bureaucracy.**

Bureaucracy's (Im)Personal Nature

Rick Warren reminds us that people are made for relationships.[1] As a part of being made in the image of God, we desire community with others. In addition to relationships, extroverts like me just like to find people to talk to, while my wife and her fellow introverts are more likely to enjoy a world of quiet retreat. So, on the boat that day, I'm really looking for people on the freighter. I could at least throw up my hand in welcome, or maybe even shout out a greeting, just to see if they could hear me over the roar of the freighter's engine. So I was pretty disappointed when no one showed!

---

[1]Rick Warren, *The Purpose Driven Life: What on Earth Am I Here For?* (Grand Rapids: Zondervan, 2002), 130.

> ■ **It's the nature of the bureaucracy that procedures, policies, written and unwritten rules, and expectations with regard to standards of behavior tend to run the organization.**

Like the freighter headed toward the ocean, bureaucratic organizations are inherently impersonal. It's not that they necessarily intend to be. It's the nature of bureaucracy that procedures, policies, written and unwritten rules, and expectations with regard to standards of behavior tend to run the organization. In other words, *nonhuman systems, not human systems,* are really in charge. Although the leaders of the organization may be great people, even great people persons, bureaucracy still leaves *little need for interpersonal relationships.* Likewise, the captain of the freighter and the crew may very well have been the nicest, most cordial folks, but I would never find out.

Bureaucracy and Adaptability

The final thing that really stood out to me was the singular focus of the freighter's mission. It surely was not out for a joyride. It was not built to do anything but go in a relatively straight path, over long distances, through potentially turbulent seas, to transport cargo to a predetermined destination. On the other hand, my little boat has much more maneuverability, which is important to me, as I like to go in to little "nooks and crannies" in the waterway, or in the lake near our home.

> ■ **Bureaucracies usually are characterized by so many layers of management that, by the time decisions are made and executed, windows of opportunity are closing.**

This suggests another way in which bureaucracies are like the freighter. They are typically so large and inflexible that the biggest danger to them could come in the need to change course quickly. The freighter would have a difficult time making a course change. A sudden shift in the depth of the waterway channel could ground the freighter with little warning.

Likewise, bureaucracies usually are characterized by so many layers of management that, by the time decisions are made and executed, windows of opportunity are closing, or even have closed.

The Little Bayliner That Could

I've heard the saying, "It takes thirteen miles to turn a battleship, but only a few feet to turn a ski boat." The lesson in that statement is that the bigger and more complex the vessel (organization), the more effort (resources) required to make a change of course. The other side of that argument is that the smaller and less-complex vessel (organization) is easier to maneuver when a course alteration is required.

■ **Adaptability, maneuverability, speed, and responsiveness are characteristic of my boat, and are some of the things usually characteristic of the innovative organization.**

That day on the water demonstrated that truth to me. That freighter, an amazing creation, does the job it's supposed to do, and does it well, while keeping everybody safe. On the other hand, my boat is much smaller, very simple and less safe, but it's a lot of fun to ride.

Bottom line, an innovative organization operates more like my small boat than like the freighter. Adaptability, maneuverability, speed, and responsiveness are characteristic of my boat, and are some of the things usually characteristic of the innovative organization.

Innovation and Infrastructure

I said earlier that innovation in a congregation is not defined by style of music, the accepted attire for those who attend worship services, or the use of drama, multimedia, etc., in the services. Rather, *an innovative approach to ministry has more to do with the way decisions are made and executed.* If we can agree on that point, then the next logical question is, *"What does innovation really look like in an organizational context?"*

Growing Inside Out

I was watching my youngest daughter recently. As we parents often do, I wondered how she would look in a few years. I tried to imagine her little body growing to maturity. After all, in just seven brief years, our youngest would be a teenager. As I was rubbing her arms, I noticed the prominence of the bone in her upper arm, and it hit me—her bones will have to grow as she grows. For some reason, I just found it hard to grasp this obvious truth—as the body grows, so does the skeletal structure (duuuuhhhh!). Another way of looking at it is that the skeletal structure must grow for the rest of the body to grow as well.

Here's the point: As my daughter grows, I will see changes that are visible on the outside of her body—her facial features will become even more beautiful than they already are, her height will probably continue to increase (she will likely overtake her vertically impaired dad in the not-too-distant future), etc. But the really cool stuff is that which I can't see!!! It is what is happening on the inside of her body that makes her grow. If we help her learn to eat and exercise in a healthy manner, she will grow in a healthy manner. If we fail to teach her well, then she will grow in an unhealthy manner. Therefore, in her growing body, the new things we see as she grows are mostly a result of new things that are happening on the inside of her body.

Creating a False Reality

As my daughter grows, she faces another option. If she so chooses, she can live an unhealthy lifestyle, but cover up the affects of that unhealthy lifestyle by artificially altering the way her body looks. This could produce a healthy appearance and give the impression that she has healthy habits. But in reality, she may not be healthy at all.

My thoughts about my daughter and her growth give rise to a couple of truths about congregations:

- *A healthy congregation is built from the inside out.* Just as with my daughter's growth, building a healthy congregation will take a long time. While I can facilitate her growth with good food and by teaching healthy habits, I cannot shortcut the process.
- A congregation can choose to take shortcuts and do those "cosmetic" things that cause it to *look healthy. However, eventually the "look" will wear off*—usually sooner than later, and things will be back to where they used to be.
- When any organization tries to shortcut a healthy growth process by "cosmetically" altering its looks, failure will be the likely outcome.

What Does Infrastructure Look Like?

In my daughter's little growing body, the skeletal structure is, in reality, her *infrastructure.* It can't be seen, as it is covered with the skin on the body. So it is with an organization. For the most part, infrastructure can't be seen, but *lasting, healthy innovation takes place in an organization's infrastructure.* The innovative organization doesn't have to promote its tendency toward innovation. Innovation just shows up in what the organization does and produces. Therefore, those looking at a congregation from the outside may never "see" the actual innovative processes in the organization. But they will see the results.

Many congregations decide that they want to become *innovative*, but don't understand the need for the inside-out change required to shift the infrastructure. They may change the style of music, or tell folks to begin dressing casually at worship, and tout themselves as an innovative church. This shortcut approach is akin to *congregational cosmetic surgery* and will not be effective over the long run. Certainly, the changes may last for a while. But if the changes haven't resulted from the reality of the congregation's identity, they could be detrimental in the congregation's life.

Infrastructure refers to the internal working of an organization. The *American Heritage Dictionary* definition is "An underlying base or foundation especially for an organization or system... The basic facilities, services, and installations needed for the functioning of a community or society, such as transportation and communications systems, water and power lines, and public institutions including schools, post offices, and prisons."

Dimensions of a Church's Infrastructure

In the congregational context, infrastructure will include at least the following dimensions of church life:

- *Human Resources* includes philosophy and procedures in things such as staffing (both paid and volunteer), and leadership development. *How people are treated* and *how people are rewarded* are major issues. Innovative congregations equip their people and help them transition into roles of service and leadership in a healthy manner.
- *Communication systems* are weak links in many congregations. The problem of insufficient levels of direct contact with members requires having to find unique ways of getting messages out to the masses. This is often a huge challenge for any congregation.
- *Technical Systems* includes all the automated/electronic devices, networks, etc., that a congregation utilizes. Often, churches have *technology gaps*. Technological innovations are often expensive, but can contribute greatly to the innovative capacity of a congregation—both in terms of infrastructure and worship style.
- *Legal Coverage* is important. Sufficient care must be taken in terms of legal liability/exposure to allow the church to operate

without being overly concerned with legal ramifications. By-laws, constitution, etc., need to reflect the way the church *best does business* and takes care of its people. *In the innovative church, the church's innovative capacity drives the content of the legal documents, and not the other way around.*

- *Foundational values* are critical to the organization. They define what is important, how the ministry and business of the church are to be carried out, what the church believes, and how folks are to treat each other. The vision and mission of the congregation are stated here.

- *Financial Systems* represent one of the highest risk areas of exposure for congregations. A church's reputation can be significantly tarnished by even one accusation of financial malfeasance. A congregation must take great care to ensure accuracy of financial records. Regular periodic review of systems and processes by external accountants helps to promote accountability for the congregation.

- *Tracking and Assimilation* of people is important. *Innovative congregations know who their people are.* They pursue information that will help them better connect members with each other and help members fulfill their desires for service within and outside the church.

- *Facilities and Grounds Management*, while absolutely necessary, often becomes the major focus of congregations. A proper perspective on facilities is a must. The innovative church understands that facilities are not a part of the vision of the church. It also understands that the *church doesn't create the spiritual wave, but that God does.* It understands that facilities simply represent a *part of the surfboard* that God has given the church as it *rides the wave.*

■ **Innovative congregations know who their people are.**

A congregation must practice innovation in each of these areas of infrastructure, and it must engrain that practice of innovation deeply in the culture of the organization *before it can begin to change its external elements.* An innovative church can be a church of any worship style, size, denomination, etc. Again, the key is the decision-making process.

Pulling It Together

So, an innovative church may be difficult to detect at first glance. An innovative approach to ministry has more to do with how decisions are made and executed. Innovative congregations will stay in touch with *external and internal environmental factors* and will have decision-making processes that (1) are *proactive* and (2) allow for *effective response* to changes in those environmental factors.

Innovation has much more to do with structure than style. So, much more, innovation has to do with flexibility and adaptability within that structure. Many church leaders don't grasp the difference. A church may appear to be innovative just because of upbeat music, casual dress, and teaching rather than preaching. But, in reality, a true innovative approach is seen at the very core of operations—the infrastructure, which is difficult to see and assess from the outside.

PART II

The Four Dimensions of Organizational Planning

Successful organizational planning is a systematic, multi-step process that involves distinct dimensions and ongoing hard work. Each dimension has its own considerations, functions, leaders, and life cycle. The straightforward, simple process I will present includes these four distinct dimensions: visionary, missional, strategic, and tactical. Understanding the process and applying it consistently within your organization will lead to a much higher degree of alignment, and will carry the organization much further toward a desirable outcome.

3

Dimension 1:
Visionary Planning

"Where Are We Going?"

Imagine jumping in your car with your teenage child. (We're imagining, so play along if you don't have one.) You start your engine, and drive off—with no intended destination in mind. You drive a while in a random pattern, making turns here and there as you feel like it. You pass the same grocery store for the second time. All of a sudden, your teen realizes that something is a little weird here.

So he asks you, *"Where are we going?"*

You reply, "I don't know. We're just riding."

We could probably venture a pretty good guess at what your teenager would say—maybe something like, *"Why, that's the dumbest thing I've heard! Why go anywhere if we don't know where we're going?"*

Chances are, you agree with your teenager's assessment of the situation. If you're like me, you could never dream of doing anything like that. Time is precious! Who has time to waste it—along with the high-priced gasoline—by riding around with no real destination in mind?

While this example is pretty obvious to us, involving real time and real money in a tangible way—i.e., driving a car—many people live their lives like this. They exert time, resources, and energy just going, going, going...with no real direction in mind. They have no destination. They are moving—but without knowing where they will end up.

Likewise, just as many individuals live like this, many organizations, including congregations, have chosen (whether they realize it or not) this type of lifestyle. Individuals and organizations like this are living with no vision—no sense of where they are going in life.

The Nature of Vision as a Driving Force

Vision must be the driving force within any organization, whether it be a congregation, business, volunteer club, etc. The organization must have a compelling picture that depicts *what could be,* and *what should be,* in the organization's future. Vision addresses the question, *"Where are we going?"*

■ **The vision must be developed and properly communicated before anything else can effectively be done.**

The vision must be developed and properly communicated before anything else can effectively be done. Everything flows from the vision. Vision comprises the framework within which decisions are made in the organization.

Visionary planning is the first dimension of organizational planning. It is the dimension from which the other three dimensions of planning flow. It has to be relevant and clear for the rest of the planning to be effective.

Much has been written about the idea of vision in the church and how it comes about. Such voluminous writing about vision has produced many different ideas about what vision is, how it comes to visionary leaders, and how these leaders communicate vision to followers. Even within a congregation, one cannot assume that the word means the same thing to any two persons—much less everyone. Leaders must take the time to carefully craft a definition of what *vision* means in the unique organization, as they must do at every dimension of the planning process. Congregations are made up of people who work vocationally in varied organizations with varied definitions of vision.

The value of corporate language in any organization is huge—often a significant part of the difference between failure and success. Pastors and leaders must model communication that is consistent. Key words must have crystal-clear meanings, so that conversations within and among the congregation can be clearly understood. A big challenge for the leader will be getting everyone on the same page with regard to their speaking the same language. A healthy and clear definition of vision can go a long way toward establishing a congregational corporate language.

The Need for Vision: What's Next?

Only a few days from the scheduled retreat, Jason Conner was really frustrated with this question he had been hearing from his people, *"What's next for our church?"* Jason knew that the church needed a direction, and not just a *to-do list* for the next year or even few months. He inherently knew that the church would have to engage in some type of planning process to find this direction. But Jason's dilemma boiled down to this: he didn't understand what effective planning was all about—mainly because he had never seen it modeled.

All the planning exercises Jason had ever been through (mainly at Antioch) had to do with the routine, day-to-day "stuff." As he thought back on those experiences, he realized that they seemed like "one and done" events. People would come together—mainly those on the deacon board, along with Jason and a few other ministry and committee leaders—and would spend a Friday night and Saturday in the fall planning out the next year for the church. *The focus was totally event-driven.* Jason realized that the only other significant planning initiative he knew of at Antioch was what was termed a "visioning process" that the church had gone through about five years before. The outcome of that initiative—one that turned out to take three years—was the new education building, a very nice facility. But once it was completed, many rooms in the facility remained under-utilized, and even empty—a fact that initially puzzled Jason. As he talked to people who had been around during that time at Antioch, Jason realized that the church had been so occupied with the building, fund-raising, etc., associated with the education building that the church had lost its focus for why the building was needed in the first place.

At Antioch, no one had ever, to Jason's knowledge, asked a question like *"What's next?"* It seems that the building and the annual calendar planning satisfied them. But now, at Creekside, folks were asking that question. In a weird way, just as the question haunted Jason, the fact that it was being asked gave him a sense of anticipation. He recognized that the Creekside leaders wanted more out of their church. They really seemed to care and were willing to go to new places and do new things. He realized that they were simply looking for him to lead them. Jason was actually beginning to think that it may be a blessing that the CCC folks were even asking the *"What's next?"* question.

Antioch Church's idea of planning was shaped, to a degree, by each of the five planning misconceptions mentioned earlier:

The *Maintenance* Approach—As a church in a maintenance mode, Antioch was naturally content with an annual calendar planning session and a building-focused "visioning" process. The major thrust at these annual sessions seemed to be on doing the same cycle of activities each year, and doing them a little better each time.

The *Big Blob* Approach—A well-meaning, caring group of people, the Antioch folks viewed planning as a single task to be done at one time. Whatever would come from the annual calendaring would constitute "the plan" for the church.

The *Once and for All* Approach—At Antioch, once a "plan" (usually from that annual calendaring session) was developed, planning was finished! For example, although the visioning process that led to the construction of the education building had been started more than ten years earlier, Antioch made no plans to initiate another planning process, other than continuing the annual calendaring sessions.

The *Mix and Match* Approach—Antioch's language around the idea of planning was very limited. Before Jason's time, during the "visioning process" that led to the facility, phrases like *visioning* and *strategic planning* seemed to be used interchangeably among the leaders. As a result, no one was clear on what planning was all about.

The *Open Invitation* Approach—While at Antioch the planning meetings weren't open to everyone, no one gave real thought in selecting who would participate. The people in certain *positions* were expected to be the ones to participate. For example, the deacon board, having traditionally been charged with administrative, management, and operational oversight functions, would be a part of the annual event. Their roles in the church caused them to focus on day-to-day operations, and so their planning activities also focused on day-to-day "stuff." As a result, they gave little thought beyond the upcoming calendar year.

While Jason himself didn't necessarily see all five deficiencies at Antioch, they were there. Looking back, he was now beginning to realize that in all the time he was there, something wasn't quite right. Could this be why he felt that, though some good things—albeit small things—were happening, he didn't sense a movement toward any real transformation? Could this be a part of the answer to his questioning why, despite having some really nice and committed people, the church seemed to have hit a plateau for the past few years? He wasn't sure about all this just yet, and he didn't have a clear picture of what should have been done at Antioch, and what should be done at Creekside. But he was certainly cataloging past experiences and getting some direction on some things *not* to do.

A Picture of Vision

One of the common misconceptions about vision is that it has to do with *action,* or what is to be done. Vision is not primarily about action. Rather, it is about a *future state of being.* It is a picture of what the individual or organization will look like at some future point.

To illustrate the idea of vision referring to a future state, I often describe vision as God sending us a snapshot of our congregation's future—a picture of how our congregation should look someday. This snapshot is one that has vivid color, with enough detail that it gives a clear direction of how to move forward.

This snapshot doesn't usually come suddenly. Rather, it comes gradually. When God gives us a vision, it usually starts out as something very foggy—perhaps so foggy that it doesn't make sense for us to even try to communicate what we are seeing.

Most people regularly dream during their sleep. Many folks can remember their dreams very vividly. Others, like me, don't remember much at all. However, with the dreams I do recall, things are quite typically foggy. I lose the details. I certainly don't want to tell people the dream because (a) my dreams almost always have missing pieces, and (b) my typical dreams don't make a lot of sense. Therefore, I'd rather not discuss those dreams I remember, for fear of appearing quite foolish. If I were to describe them, folks would laugh and shoot holes in my dreams with their ridicule (and I don't blame them).

That snapshot God downloads to us has the same appearance. When we first catch a glimpse, it is truly foggy. It is not easy to see, much less comprehend, what it is trying to say to us. It takes time for us to zero in on the snapshot so that we can begin seeing things more clearly. Likewise, in the early stages of the vision, we may be very guarded about sharing it with any one. As with our dreams, we know they may sound foolish and others may shoot holes in the vision.

Eventually, if we pay attention, the vision God sends will become clearer. That snapshot, foggy at first, will ultimately have high resolution and will be quite vivid. However, we have to keep in mind that downloading a large, high-resolution photo to a computer takes a long time. So is usually the case with a vision from God.

The Birth of a Vision

God typically gives a vision over time, as the organization goes through ups and downs, successes and mistakes, and learns lessons along the way. A common misconception about vision is that *God gives it with a bolt of lightning*—whoosh! One second it's not there, and the next second it is. But that's not how it usually works. God often communicates vision through stages—stages not always characterized by triumph and success, but often by failure and heartache.

Perhaps the best biblical picture of this is found in Nehemiah's story. God gave him a vision concerning what could, and should be in Jerusalem. The city lay in near ruins due to the Babylonian siege nearly 150 years earlier, along with the subsequent neglect since that time. God revealed to Nehemiah the vision for rebuilding the walls of the city, but it's as if He did it in stages.

Stage 1: Vision Is Birthed from an Obstacle

Nehemiah was in Babylon, in the service of the Persian king Artaxerxes, as his cupbearer, or "taste-tester." If anyone tried to poison the king, Nehemiah would be the one to "take the hit" for the king. This speaks to the character of Nehemiah, as the cupbearer would have to be among the most trusted of the king's servants.

Nehemiah begins his story in chapter 1 by telling us that his own brother, Hanani, and a group of men had just returned from a long road trip to Judah. When Nehemiah asked how things were in Jerusalem, the reply was not all that good: "They said to me, 'Things are not going well for those who returned to the province of Judah. They are in great trouble and disgrace. The wall of Jerusalem has been torn down, and the gates have been destroyed by fire'" (Neh. 1:3).

■   **A vision often starts with an obstacle.**

The news had a profound effect on Nehemiah. Being a trusted servant of the king, he knew of the government's willingness to allow Jews to return to their homeland, a place that Nehemiah had never even seen. God had obviously given Nehemiah a real passion for the resettling of Jerusalem. But Nehemiah saw the broken down nature of the city for what it was—an obstacle. It was an obstacle to the fulfillment of something that was important to Nehemiah's people.

A vision often starts with an obstacle. God often uses an obstacle to cause someone to begin thinking in a particular direction.

Stage 2: The Obstacle Becomes a Burden

Nehemiah's next move is kind of heart-wrenching: "When I heard this, I sat down and wept. In fact, for days I mourned, fasted, and prayed to the God of heaven" (Neh. 1:4).

In Nehemiah's mind and heart, this obstacle of the walls being broken down would become a full-blown *burden*—a heavy one, at that! *Burden* is one of those "churchy words" that tend to get overused in the language of religiosity. But this situation calls for a heavy word to describe a really heavy heart. The *American Heritage Dictionary* defines *burden* as "Something that is emotionally difficult to bear; A source of great worry or stress; weight…"

This feeling of heaviness caused Nehemiah to take some fairly drastic measures. He spent lots of time before God, crying his heart out and fasting, all the time praying to God for direction. Nehemiah's burden emerged from seeing the gap separating what was, *what could be*, and *what should be*.

Stage 3: The Burden Becomes a Passion

Nehemiah's burden for the city of Jerusalem and his people continued to grow until it became what seemed like an obsession for him. His prayers to God took on an even greater sense of desperation:

> Then I said, "O LORD, God of heaven, the great and awesome God who keeps his covenant of unfailing love with those who love him and obey his commands, listen to my prayer! Look down and see me praying night and day for your people Israel. I confess that we have sinned against you. Yes, even my own family and I have sinned! We have sinned terribly by not obeying the commands, decrees, and regulations that you gave us through your servant Moses." (Neh. 1:5–7)

Passion is a concept that is really hard for us to grasp nowadays. In the world of Christianity, we are encouraged to find our passion and to live into it. Our passion is to drive us—motivate us—in discovering God's plan for our lives. I buy in to all of that. But how can we define *passion*? Turning to the *American Heritage Dictionary* again, we find this definition: "A powerful emotion, such as love, joy, hatred, or anger… Ardent love… Boundless enthusiasm."

Nehemiah's prayer reveals strong emotion, great love for his homeland and his people, and what would ultimately be a boundless enthusiasm, a willingness to make happen what he was praying about. His burden had clearly become a passion.

But how do we know when that movement from burden to passion has taken place? It will look different for different people, based on their personality, temperament, level of initiative, etc. A general rule of thumb says: *A burden becomes a passion when (a) you just can't shake it, and (b) you become consumed with the idea of doing something about it."*

Nehemiah prayed and fasted for days and days—we don't know how long. He just couldn't shake it. What he had learned about the state of Jerusalem tore him apart. He went a step further. He was ready to do something about it. He realized that the sins of his ancestors had caused the city to be besieged and the ancestors to be uprooted. God was just in allowing the Babylonians to take over Judah, just as He had been just in allowing the Assyrians to take the Northern Kingdom, Israel. So Nehemiah went right to the heart of the issue: In his prayer, he asked God to allow him to take the responsibility of the sins of his people (v. 6–7).

Stage 4: Passion Clarifies the Opportunity

A further key to visionary thinking is to move beyond seeing problems as obstacles and to begin seeing them as opportunities. A glass filled halfway with water provides the standard illustration. One person may see the glass as half-empty. We label this person a pessimist, someone who doesn't see that anything can be done to make the situation any different. Another may see the glass as half-full. We call this person an optimist, or perhaps an opportunist, who sees the situation in a positive light, as something that can be enhanced.

■ **A key to visionary thinking is to move beyond seeing problems as obstacles, and to begin seeing them as opportunities.**

So far, Nehemiah sees the obstacle that the broken-down city presents to the resettlement of Jerusalem. Then he senses the critical nature of the situation and pours his heart out to God about it. Third, somewhere in between feeling the pressure of an almost impossible situation in Jerusalem, and taking responsibility for his people's sins, Nehemiah realizes that this burden won't go away. It becomes a passion—almost an obsession. Finally, he captures the sense that he can, and is called to, do something about the situation. And so he decides to do just that. "O Lord, please hear my prayer! Listen to the prayers of those of us who delight in honoring you. Please grant me success today by making the king favorable to me. Put it into his heart to be kind to me." (Neh. 1:11).

The process is complete. The *obstacle* has now become, in Nehemiah's heart and mind, an *opportunity*! Somewhere along the line, after hearing from his brother and his friends about the destruction in Jerusalem, and the problems it posed to the re-settlement of the area, Nehemiah internalized the situation, and took ownership. The result is—something needs to be done, and Nehemiah is compelled to do it.

Do "Visions" Make Sense?

Often, when God communicates a vision, it seems kind of wacky. God gave Nehemiah what seemed to be an unlikely vision, due to a number of things:

- As far as we know, Nehemiah had never been to the Jerusalem area.
- The area around Jerusalem was largely poor. Even the Jews who had returned still experienced great poverty. Very few businesses would have been started.
- The folks who had moved back to Jerusalem would not have necessarily constituted a skilled work force.
- Jerusalem's interior location in the hills made it difficult to acquire building materials.
- Many influential non-Jews living in and around the Jerusalem region did not want the city to be rebuilt. A revived independent Jerusalem would surely threaten the Persian empire and the hefty taxes collected in the town. Nehemiah would face stiff opposition.

A Closely Held Dream

For the most part, Nehemiah kept his dream to himself, largely a secret, until the right time. He didn't feel the need to tell anyone about it—except, of course, the king, whose support would be absolutely necessary. Nehemiah was obviously a very secure person—one who didn't need to let folks know what God was giving him to do. For days he kept what God had given him in his own mind and heart.

Nehemiah's discretion can teach us much. When we catch an idea we are excited about, we want to rush out to tell other people. When we do that, we may get this look that suggests, *"You need to be carried away in a straight jacket to the 'funny farm.'"* As a *dreamer* who thinks and talks in visionary terms, I know those looks, because I often get them.

Herein lies a dilemma for those of us who get "Nehemiah-type" ideas: When we get these ideas, we often need someone to help us process them. We need people to hear us; people we know we can trust and who will be patient with us, who won't laugh hysterically when we tell them what we're thinking.

A good rule of thumb for the dreamer to remember is this: *The bigger the vision, the less you can say about it*—at least in the infancy of the vision. Nehemiah waited for days before he would even approach the king with his idea and his request. During that time, a vision, which had initially been foggy, got clearer. He could then communicate it much better than when God first began to download the photograph.

One of the most important skills dreamers can develop is the ability to *anticipate the questions* their ideas will generate in others. This takes a great deal of discernment and the ability to evaluate critically one's own ideas. This ability is also a function of one's maturity. To have the ability to be honest with oneself, a dreamer must be secure enough in who he or she is and in what he or she is called to do. Often, less-mature people can't evaluate their own ideas critically. Their sensitivities override their better judgment.

■ **A good rule of thumb for the dreamer: the bigger the vision, the less you can say about it—at least in the infancy of the vision.**

To get to the questions others may ask, the dreamer may ask himself questions:

- What are the perspectives held by the people who will likely hear about my vision?
- What is it about the vision that will threaten their perspectives?
- What about the vision is sensational? Wacky?
- What about the vision seems like an impossibility?

Once the anticipated questions are identified, it would be good for the dreamer to discuss the vision with a trusted friend or associate and incorporate these questions and answers into a discussion about the vision.

Vision's "Ownership Value"

Ownership of the vision is a high value in the innovative congregation. Without the members owning the vision, the congregation has little hope of ever seeing it fulfilled. You can build this ownership among the members in at least two distinct ways.

First, *ownership can come during the process of vision development, if leadership is sensitive to who participates in the process.* Congregational leadership needs to strategically enlist the participants from among those committed members who seem to be dreamers, or *big picture people.* This group should include the lead pastor, even if he is not a dreamer.

Many congregations assume *the pastor is naturally a dreamer.* This expectation comes from the assumption that when God equips someone as a pastor, He must always equip a visionary. Such logic is faulty. Many capable and effective pastors don't have a visionary tendency. Some are simply not dreamers. The lofty, false expectations that come with the position of pastor put many into a precarious situation. Feeling the pressure, they may try to *manufacture a vision* and try to lead the church with whatever they can generate and pass off as vision.

At the other extreme lies the church so driven by congregational leadership it doesn't even want the pastor involved in visionary planning. The assumption here may sound something like this, *"We were here before Pastor Jon came, and we'll still be here after he leaves!"* This can be quite frustrating for any pastor. Sadly, entire denominations have polity built on this idea.

Unfortunately, neither of these churches will be able to see the unique vision that God has for it. As a result, they will probably settle for a counterfeit vision rather than the real vision God has in mind.

■ **There are many capable and effective pastors who don't have a visionary tendency.**

The Visionary Conduit

The congregation needs to discern the *visionary conduit* that God has placed in the church. By *visionary conduit* I refer to whatever group of committed people God has equipped with a gift/tendency to discern the big picture view of what God wants the church to be. Sometimes the pastor is a clear visionary. Quite often the opposite is true. In those cases, the church must seek to discover the visionary laypeople and put them to work.

Effective communication of the vision can drive ownership among the members. This can happen after enough of the snapshot comes into view that the vision is relatively clear and questions can be answered. At this point the vision can be communicated. Communication of the vision has to be done with great care. In a congregation, the vision needs to be continually communicated for the purposes of *information, clarification, and motivation.*

The Vision: Statement or Story

Many organizations use what they refer to as a *vision statement.* In the past few decades a prevailing idea among American organizations has been to have vision statements that are brief so that employees, members, etc., can memorize and recite them whenever necessary. Many congregations, too, have adopted these brief vision statements.

■ **If your vision can be written out in less than a couple of pages, it's probably not really a vision.**

The idea of a brief vision statement is almost an oxymoron. If the vision that a congregation adopts is truly clear, if that download of the snapshot that gives the picture of the future is really clear, then how can it be summarized in a single statement? A clear vision from God would have to be communicated more as a newspaper story, or perhaps an entire newspaper section. If your vision can be written out in less than a couple of pages, it's probably not really a vision.

The Visionary Life Cycle

In the life of any organization, *change is inevitable.* Healthy organizations "manage" the change, so that they can achieve a competitive advantage. In a healthy church, life cycles will be associated with vision. Leaders will realize that at times God will give new vision, and with new vision comes new opportunities.

Over time, a vision can "run dry." Great excitement usually surrounds a well-articulated vision in the early years after its introduction, but that excitement can wane as time goes on. The case is often that "newness motivates"! Along with other experts, Church Health Consultant George Bullard, in a part of his Spiritual Strategic Journey process, notes that vision needs to be renewed at least every seven to ten years or so. This far into a vision's life cycle, one of three situations are likely to have arisen:

Insufficient progress has been made toward the vision's fulfillment, and it becomes obvious that it simply won't happen. In this situation, it's best for the organization to be honest about the situation, perhaps start all over and seek a new vision.

The vision has been fulfilled.

Significant progress has been made toward the stated vision, and "staying the course" will most likely lead to its fulfillment. But the leaders—the "go-getters" in the congregation—need a new challenge. In this situation, a new vision needs to be articulated even before the prior vision is fulfilled.

From Photo to the Canvas

I love to use the snapshot picture to illustrate vision to our congregation. However, the photo is just a starting point. We must remember that getting a handle on the vision is only a part of the game. Once the vision is adequately clear, it must be executed. For the second part of the equation, I tell our folks that God also provides a canvas—one suitable for painting. Along with that canvas He provides a paintbrush for each member of the congregation. As the snapshot becomes clearer through (hopefully) effective communication by the leadership, each of us are to pick up our brush and paint a few strokes—representing our contribution to the fulfillment of the vision. This is a picture of 1 Corinthians 12, as the brush strokes line up with our unique role in the body of Christ.

The result is, over time, a reproduction of that original snapshot, with contributions by as many as possible in the body. The participants also are much more likely to *own* the vision! Why? Because they helped to paint the picture.

But how do the participants actually "stroke the canvas"? What does that look like? How do they really get involved? That's where the next three dimensions of planning come in.

Putting It All Together

Vision must be the driving force within any organization. *A vision is a compelling picture that depicts what could be, and what should be, in the organization's future.* It addresses the question, *"Where are we going?"* A vision usually comes over time, often through experience.

A real vision captures the energy of the organization's members, and they mobilize together to fulfill it. Over time, however, a vision can *run dry*, and leadership will be challenged to *keep it fresh*. An innovative church will recognize that God may use multiple members as conduits through whom He communicates vision for the congregation.

4

Dimension 2:
Missional Planning

"What Will We Do on the Way?"

Recently I addressed a group of church planters on *"My Top Ten Lessons from the First Ten Years."* The idea was to share with them my mistakes and learnings from the first ten years of our church's life, in hopes that the "school of hard knocks" would not have to be quite so tough on them.

On one of the ten points, I struck a nerve. You could have heard a pin drop on a carpeted floor. The statement, I knew, was so radically opposed to what they had read in books and had been hearing in the conferences they attended.

Overrating Vision

"Vision is overrated!"

■ **"Vision is overrated!"**

Blank stares. Mouths dropping open. I had trampled on the sacred ground that had been created for our church planters. The reaction was so profound that I truly didn't know whether to (a) continue with my point or (b) copout, laugh, and say something like, *"Ha! Just wanted to see if you're still with me…"*

But, I chose to continue. The point? Vision *is* overrated, in many organizations, for two reasons.

First, vision is a *catchy concept* —particularly in congregational life. It is seen as a panacea in many churches. Having strong vision, it is said, can overcome many deficiencies and grow a healthy church. But, there's much more to it than that. For one thing, definitions of vision are all over the map. Settling on a common understanding of vision will be a huge challenge for a congregation, or any organization, for that matter.

The second reason is perhaps more understandable: Vision can overwhelm people—the very people it is intended to inspire—when it is not accompanied by a "roadmap" for the vision to be realized. A vision does have a life cycle. But a vision can never really begin until it gets some traction in an organization. Traction occurs when those in the organization can get a handle on what the vision is about, and they can see enough of it so that they feel some energy around it.

■ **Vision can overwhelm people—the very people it is intended to inspire—when it is not accompanied by a "roadmap" for the vision to be realized.**

We have to remember that a vision is, in fact, a dream. Remember our look at Nehemiah in the previous chapter? A dream often doesn't make sense—perhaps even to the one dreaming it. If I were to tell you about a dream I had while sleeping, you may either laugh uncontrollably or look at me with a blank stare. You may wait for me to give you some clarification that addresses the natural questions: *"So what?"* *"What does this matter to me?"* and so on. But I may not be able to provide any more information for you. Maybe the dream was so crazy that even I didn't understand it. The point is this—the vision is not enough. To many people, vision is simply crazy.

■ **Many people simply don't have perspective that allows them to fully grasp that big picture.**

Likewise, it is important that leaders understand that, even when they have in their minds a vision that is fairly clear, communicating it over and over is simply not enough. Many people simply don't have perspective that allows them to fully grasp that big picture. They need more. They need vision casters to come down from their 35,000 foot altitude, and help them see it at 20,000, and even 10,000 and 5,000 feet. The not-so-good news comes in two forms: (a) many vision casters are incapable of coming down from the 35,000 foot altitude, and (b) many in the typical organization simply don't have the big picture perspective and can't understand even a simplified vision talk. The good news is this: even those people *do* have *a* perspective! The challenge for the leader is becoming aware of that perspective, helping the individuals become aware of that perspective, and plugging them in to the planning process at a level that capitalizes on that perspective.

Developing the Roadmap

I don't rely on roadmaps that much. I guess I'm just that typical American male who thinks it's a waste of time (and a blow to the ego) to stop and ask someone, or to read a map, for directions. For example, we recently purchased a used vehicle that has the OnStar capability, and I didn't even consider purchasing the subscription for directions. I guess it's just too much like stopping to ask. When I make a road trip, an inherent assumption is made: *the destination actually exists*. However, although I know the destination exists, I may not know the way there. I can take one of two general approaches—both of which are exemplified in two of my all-time favorite movies.

The "Jake and Elwood Blues" Approach

The first approach I call the "Jake and Elwood Blues" (or the "wing it") approach. I name this for the classic film *The Blues Brothers*. Jake and Elwood Blues, recently released from prison, caught a vision of sorts—they knew they were to save an orphanage that was facing foreclosure. Now Jake and Elwood didn't know a lot about what they were doing, other than they were on *"a mission from God."* Driven by the desire to save the orphanage (good boys, those Blues Brothers!), they had no idea how to raise the money, or how they would get the money to the orphanage once they raised it. They had a destination, but they had no roadmap on how to get there.

Many congregations take the "Jake and Elwood" approach. They value the idea of reaching the destination, but they have difficulty thinking through how to actually make it to that destination. These congregations do little planning and place little emphasis on making sure everyone is involved in a way that maximizes the effectiveness of the congregation. The result is that they "wing it"—just like the Blues Brothers.

However, many "wing it" congregations figure that they, like Jake and Elwood, will reach that destination, despite winging it. (Of course, the Blues Brothers' rescue of the orphanage has less to do with reality and more to do with theatrics). Still, congregations may reach their destiny, like Jake and Elwood, by leaving significant destruction in their wake.

Churches using the "Jake and Elwood" approach may be all about vision. They may be able to sense God's direction and destination, internalize it, and even communicate it. Yet if they can't translate it into something that the majority of the organization can ultimately buy in to, they may never get beyond that stage of communication. This is where the roadmap comes in. It will help the organization members grasp not only where they need to go, but what they must do to get there.

The Clark W. Griswold Approach

The second approach I call the "Clark W. Griswold" approach. In the National Lampoon series of *Vacation* films, Chevy Chase plays the role of a committed, but nerdish, dad who obviously has control issues. Even when it comes to vacation time, Clark maps everything out to the "nth" degree. His meticulous approach to planning the trip out becomes more important than the trip itself. In the detail of his preparation, he forgets the big picture and makes the vacation all about the overly detailed plan. His approach to planning things out suppresses the fun and leads to a miserable trip for his family!

Many organizations employ the "Clark W. Griswold" approach. They focus on the details so much that they lose sight of the big picture. As with Clark, it's easier to control the short intermediate steps depicted on the roadmap. Organizations like this often become bureaucracies, in which rules, hierarchy, and control are among the unwritten prevailing values.

What Does a Roadmap Look Like?

Vision must be the driving force in the successful organization. Vision can be the force that creates positive momentum. But momentum has to be sustained on a regular basis. The idea of momentum can be likened to the revolutions of a large flywheel. In his ground-breaking book, *Good to Great,* Stanford professor and business guru Jim Collins writes:

> Picture a huge, heavy flywheel—a massive metal disk mounted horizontally on an axle, about 30 feet in diameter, 2 feet thick, and weighing about 5,000 pounds. Now imagine that your task is to get the flywheel rotating on the axle as fast and long as possible.

Pushing with great effort, you get the flywheel to inch forward, moving almost imperceptibly at first. You keep pushing, and after two or three hours of persistent effort, you move it around a second rotation. You keep pushing in a consistent direction…

Then, at some point—breakthrough! The momentum of the thing kicks in your favor, hurling the flywheel forward, turn after turn…whoosh!…its own heavy weight working for you. You're pushing no harder than during the first rotation, but the flywheel goes faster and faster. Each turn of the flywheel builds upon work done earlier, compounding your investment of effort. A thousand times faster, then ten thousand, then a hundred thousand. The huge heavy disk flies forward, with almost unstoppable momentum.

Now suppose someone came along and asked, "What was the one big push that caused this thing to go so fast?"

You wouldn't be able to answer… Was it the first push? The second? The fifth? The hundredth? No, it was all of them added together in an overall accumulation of the effort applied in a consistent direction…

No matter how dramatic the end result, the good-to-great transformations never happened in one fell swoop. There was no single defining action, no grand program, no one killer innovation, no solitary lucky break, no wrenching revolution. Good to great comes about by a cumulative process—step by step, action by action, decision by decision, turn by turn of the flywheel—that adds up to sustained and spectacular results.[1]

While a compelling vision can certainly get the flywheel going, it takes successful progress toward the realization of the vision to keep it turning, and at an ever-increasing pace. Here the roadmap comes in. A well laid out roadmap can give organizational members the confidence and security they need, and can help them see better where they fit in to the big picture. The roadmap can also give direction on how to obtain "small successes" that create momentum and keep the flywheel turning.

---

[1] Jim Collins, *Good to Great* (New York: HarperCollins, 2001), 164–65.

The "Drive" of Vision

Vision is all about answering the question, *"Where are we going?"* It is about *what is to be*. It is about the destination. As the driving force in an organization, the question becomes *"What does the vision drive?"* Simply put, the vision drives the second dimension of organizational planning, which I call *missional planning*. The term *missional*, as used in this context, differs from the use of the word in terms of the missional movement among evangelical churches. This missional movement is grounded in the Great Commission in Matthew 28:19–20, which records Jesus' words just before He ascended to heaven: "Therefore go and make disciples of all nations, baptizing them in the name of the Father and of the Son and of the Holy Spirit, and teaching them to obey everything I have commanded you. And surely I am with you always, to the very end of the age" (NIV).

The missional movement among churches emphasizes going beyond the church walls to make disciples, meeting people where they actually are, to meet their needs with the Gospel of Christ. The missional movement is based on the premise of Jesus' command—to influence people *as we are going* along our way.

Missional Planning: What Is It?

As visionary planning deals with the question, *"Where are we going?"* missional planning addresses the question, "What *will we do while we are on the way* to that destination defined by the vision?" Simply put—the vision is all about what *is to be*. The mission is about what *is to be done* to bring the vision to reality.

The Mission Statement

Many, if not most, organizations use mission statements to get a message across to their employees and customers. The typical mission statement in most organizations can be defined as *a statement that lays out, in a very broad sense, what the organization does*. In most organizations, the mission statement is relatively brief so it may be easier to recall. But beyond that, particularly in congregations, there seems to be little consensus on what a mission statement is and what it is to communicate.

Mission: Impossible (?)

As a kid, I watched the popular *Mission: Impossible* television series. Now *that* was great TV! Every show had a couple of elements that were consistent from week-to-week. At the beginning of each episode, Peter Graves & co. would receive a recorded message from an inconspicuously located cassette player. The message was intended to communicate to the team the latest assignment—one that invariably would carry a high degree of risk. Once the message was communicated, the tape would self-destruct.

A "designed for television" characteristic of the show is worth noting. The assigned mission was always accomplished by the end of the episode so a brand new mission could be communicated to the team the next week.

What I love about this show is its illustration of three clear points about mission. First, a mission *must have an action orientation.* Mission deals with the issue of what *needs to be done* for the vision—*what is to be*—to be fulfilled. Thus mission requires action. In addition, any statement about mission must incorporate a sense of that action. Mission is, then, very "verb-intensive."

> ■ **Mission must have an action orientation.**

Second, a mission must have a *completion point.* Just as the *MI* series cast completed their mission each week, a mission, to be successful, must be completed! Unfortunately, many missions in many organizations are stated without any sign of a completion point. Without a completion point, how can a team know whether they are being successful in fulfilling that mission?

> ■ **A mission must have a completion point.**

Third, to be successful, the mission should be tailored to the *uniqueness* of the team or organization charged with carrying it out. The *MI* team was quite specialized. Its assignments spoke to the already-established strengths of the team and the team members. Because the assignments were tailored to those strengths, the team was nearly always successful! Different teams and organizations have different strengths. They should focus on tackling challenges that they are equipped to handle.

> ■ **The mission should be tailored to the uniqueness of the team or organization charged with carrying it out.**

An Integrity Church Story

A situation that arose in our congregation clearly illustrated to me these three points about mission.

About six years ago our church was still recovering from a significant "train wreck" (the first of two in our eleven-year history), as I like to call it. A doctrinal division led to the loss of over twenty-five families, a significant number in a two-year-old church of maybe four hundred people. Many of these were ministry leaders who had been convinced that the *Purpose Driven methodology* under which we had started our church was unbiblical and that I was a leader who was unable to minister to hurting people who had begun attending our church.

So, for over a couple of years our church had been somewhat adrift with little or no direction. We really were not driven by any sense of vision or mission, as we had fallen into a maintenance/ recovery mode. Our focus during that time was on healing.

As we reached what we thought was a sufficient level of recovery, I decided that we should develop a new mission statement for our church. My idea was that an effective statement could help to motivate our people by driving greater energy and ownership. So we worked with leaders over a period of a couple of months or so, and came up with a pretty good statement: *"Our mission is to develop fully devoted followers of Jesus Christ."*

Our statement really worked for a while. We had refrigerator magnets made, posters hung around the facilities, etc. Folks resonated with it at first. However, over time, it seemed to have lost its pizzazz. After only about a year or so, it didn't seem to motivate anymore.

I wracked my brain trying to figure this out. I knew our statement was as biblical as could be. But it wasn't having a great impact! Later I really began to understand the true nature of mission. Then I realized what had happened. The mission statement we had adopted violated the three points of mission described above. I realized then that what we had wasn't a mission statement at all.

Action, Completion Point, and Uniqueness Needed

The first obvious point about the statement is that *it didn't really have an action orientation*. It said very little, or nothing, about the *action* that would be required to actually develop fully devoted followers of Christ. Now, a mission statement doesn't have to be really specific. But it does have to be focused. I like to say that a mission is a *broad course for action*.

Second, I realized that our statement had *no completion point*. We called it a mission statement, but the statement itself was couched in such a way that it didn't provide a "benchmark" for knowing whether or not we were successful at any given point. It's true that Jesus never gave us the option of having a completion point when it comes to developing fully devoted followers. Particularly in discourses such as the parable of the talents in Matthew 25, He emphasizes that mandate to stay faithful to our assigned responsibilities until His return. In our *MI* show analogy, the mission communicated to Graves & co. gave a clear picture of what "mission accomplished" would look like. Our statement, unfortunately, gave our church no such thing.

Reggie Joiner, Lane Jones, and Andy Stanley place a big emphasis on "clarifying the win." Clarifying the win is the process that leads to the definition of "mission accomplished." Joiner, Jones, and Stanley write:

> Clarifying the win simply means communicating to your team what is really important and what really matters. Asking certain questions, rewarding an individual's performance, celebrating significant outcomes—these are all part of clarifying the win. Practicing this principle means that you are intentional about defining a win so that you don't accidentally communicate the wrong win or keep your team guessing about what is really important.[2]

The statement of the congregation's mission should always keep in view the definition of "the win" and give a clear picture of what success and "mission accomplished" really look like. Unfortunately, ours didn't.

The third problem with our mission statement was *its generality*. The statement itself was very good—it was biblical, relevant, and even very powerful. I mean, that's what Jesus was—and is—all about: making disciples! The statement meant a lot to others outside our church as well. From many of those we heard comments such as, *"That's what we need to be doing too!"* They realized that this statement could, and should, be theirs as well. As a matter of fact, that was the nature of the third problem: While our statement was biblical, relevant, and powerful, it spoke nothing to the unique nature of our church. While it grabbed our people at the level of biblical veracity, it would not capture the energy of our folks, simply because it didn't give enough on how to expend that energy.

When God gives a mission, he takes into account the uniqueness with which He created us. Ephesians 2:10 is pretty clear on this: "For we are God's masterpiece. He has created us anew in Christ Jesus, so that we can do the good things he planned for us long ago."

---

[2]Andy Stanley, Reggie Joiner, Lane Jones, *7 Practices of Effective Ministry* (Sisters, Oreg.: Multnomah, 2004), 71–72.

However, our mission statement did not take into account anything about our uniqueness as a church, or the uniqueness of the individuals that make up the church family.

■ **What we had crafted a few years back was not really a mission statement after all. Rather, it was a purpose statement.**

In the end we recognized that the lack of action orientation, a completion point, and a focus on our uniqueness didn't negate the value of the statement. But it made me realize that what we had crafted a few years back was not really a mission statement after all. Rather, it was a *Purpose Statement*. You see, the statement was very valid. It was driven by what may very well be the most important passages Jesus ever gave us:

> Jesus replied, "You must love the Lord your God with all your heart, all your soul, and all your mind.' This is the first and greatest commandment. A second is equally important: 'Love your neighbor as yourself." (Mt. 22:37–39)

> "Therefore, go and make disciples of all the nations, baptizing them in the name of the Father and the Son and the Holy Spirit. Teach these new disciples to obey all the commands I have given you. And be sure of this: I am with you always, even to the end of the age." (Mt. 28:19–20)

Purpose: A New Wrinkle

Both vision and mission must speak to the uniqueness of the organization. Otherwise, as we have discussed, they won't capture the imagination and energy of the organization. In congregational life, certain commands, directives, etc., are so fundamental in fulfilling God's plan for the church that we can reasonably say that they apply to all churches that claim to follow Jesus. In other words, very few churches, regardless of their context, uniqueness, etc., would say that the Great Commandment and Great Commission don't apply to them.

■ **Purpose can be described as the biblical mandate that God has ordained for the church as a whole—the universal church. Because the mandate is for the universal church, it applies to every congregation, regardless of context, uniqueness, etc.**

Purpose can be described as the biblical mandate that God has ordained for the church as a whole—the universal church. Because the mandate is for the universal church, it applies to every congregation, regardless of context, uniqueness, etc. This really began to strike at me when I heard people in other churches comment that the mission statement we had adopted sounded good to them and applied to them just as it did for us.

The Missional Life Cycle

As stated in the previous chapter, an effective vision will have a typical life cycle of 7–10 years. By this time in the life of the vision, it is pretty obvious to those in the organization that either (a) it has been fulfilled, (b) it won't be fulfilled, or (c) sufficient progress has been made so that its fulfillment is inevitable. So, every 7–10 years the organizational vision needs to be renewed.

But what happens to the mission when the visionary life cycle is completed—when the vision needs to be renewed? Just as a vision has a life cycle, so does a mission.

Multiple Missions

A healthy and relevant vision will be comprehensive. The healthy vision will lay out an ever-clearing picture of a destination—a new future state that will require action. A number of things will need to happen for the complete visionary picture to be replicated. Just as our friends in the *MI* television series demonstrated, fulfillment of a vision will require numerous actions—some quite complex and others quite simple. *Multiple missions will likely be required* during a visionary life cycle.

The typical working definition of a "mission statement" is something like this: *a statement that lays out, in a very broad sense, what the organization does.* In most organizations, that statement, by design, never changes. It is typically intended to keep employees focused on how to go about their business in fulfilling the organization's business and to communicate to the customer the commitment of the organization to the satisfaction of that customer.

However, the idea of a mission that is designed to accomplish major pieces of a larger visionary picture challenges the typical view of mission as a static statement that doesn't change over time. For a mission to be truly effective, it must, as we said earlier, be action-oriented, have a completion point, and be unique to the organization in which it applies. All three of these criteria point to the premise that a mission, and therefore a mission statement, is temporary. A mission, then, is temporary in that it addresses the broad course for action in effect between the time the mission begins and the time it is completed.

Based on this definition, *an organization will likely have multiple missions in effect during a visionary life cycle,* as multiple courses for action will be required to bring about necessary changes. Instead of one major statement focusing on the organization's mission, multiple statements will clarify multiple missions. These missions will be carried out either simultaneously or sequentially.

Mission or Missions?

If vision fulfillment requires multiple missions during the course of the visionary life cycle, then a relevant question for the organization becomes, *"How many missions can one organization handle?"* This question addresses the issue of resource availability within the organization. The resource pool the question typically addresses is that of "human resources." Obviously, the larger the pool of competent and experienced people at the organization's disposal, the greater the number of missions the organization can handle. In addition, the resource availability issue drives the question of whether the organization can even consider pursuing multiple missions simultaneously.

■ **There will be multiple missions in effect during a visionary life cycle, as multiple courses for action will be required in order to bring about necessary changes.**

Berea Church: Its Vision and Mission

Before we go too much deeper into this topic, an example is in order. During a recent seminar, a pastor in attendance asked what a mission might look like. I asked him if we could take his church as an example. He agreed, but he admitted that his church didn't have a clear vision at this point. After I asked a few "coaching" questions of the pastor, he came up with the idea of his church—let's call it *Berea Church*—wanting to become the *"leading multicultural ministry in our region of the state."* While Berea, at this time, was an almost completely white congregation, it was located in perhaps one of the most ethnically diverse counties in our state. He knew that for Berea to be relevant, it would have to tap in to the changing demographics in the area.

With the idea of becoming the *"leading multicultural ministry in our region of the state"* as a very brief and incomplete summary statement of the church's vision, we set out to look for the possible "missional thrusts" that could result in the fulfillment of the vision.

First, we looked at the vision to determine its major focal point. *"What are the most critical shifts that must occur for the vision to become reality?"* In Berea's case, a move from *"monoculturalism"* to *multiculturalism* is the key shift that would propel the church toward fulfillment of its vision.

The second question might be, *"What can we do to make that shift occur?"* In Berea's situation, the shift would most likely have to be catalyzed at the level of each of the ethnic groups in its geographic area. These multiple cultures, then, would best be defined by the three most prominent ethnic groups (besides European Americans)— Native Americans, Hispanics, and African Americans—in that county.

The next natural step is to address the framing of the mission(s). In this case, Berea has to be focused on each of previously "unreached" ethnic groups in its region. Therefore, it would be healthy to build the mission around these ethnic groups, and what reaching these groups would accomplish in Berea Church and in the surrounding community.

An effective "missional framework" would be, then, to structure three distinct, but common, missions around these three ethnic groups. The missions that may come out of this process may look something like this:

Mission 1: To build a substantial population of Hispanics into the Berea church family.

Mission 2: To build a substantial population of African Americans into the Berea church family.

Mission 3: To build a substantial population of Indian Americans into the Berea church family.

Note that each of the three mission statements are essentially the same, with the exception of the three target ethnic groups being specified. That is because, in terms of what Berea must *do* to become the *leading multicultural ministry in our region of the state*, the broad course for action is essentially the same. Because of the uniqueness of each ethnic group, there will, however, be different strategies that will apply to each of the three groups. But at the missional level, a common statement can apply to the three distinct groups.

The Test of the Mission(s)

Now, let's test the three mission statements against our three criteria, to see how they rate as true missional thrusts.

First, *are the statements action-oriented?* For the most part, yes. The wording "…to build…" implies the development of something from nothing to a substantial presence. For example, when I go back and look at the pictures of the land on which our house was built, I am amazed at the difference between today and twenty-five years ago, when one-and-three-fourths acres were covered with scrub pines. While Berea's mission statements are actionable, as the planning process goes further, the congregation may need to identify more specific action steps with actionable language.

Second, *does the mission imply a completion point?* Of course, we know that in a congregational sense we can never stop trying to reach people, even those in different target ethnic groups. At the same time, any truly innovative church will recognize that their particular church won't reach everybody. Rather, in today's America, the truly innovative church will target those that it is best equipped to reach, based on geographic and demographic factors, as well as issues of congregational strength.

With regard to a completion point, the words "…substantial population…" are significant. Berea may determine that the mission's completion point is reached when there exists a sizable number of that ethnic group functioning and contributing within the Berea church body. The church may even want, for example, to clarify the mission further by setting a goal of *building this significant population into the church with 20 percent of that ethnic population in the county.*

The third criteria of *uniqueness is perhaps more easily seen with Berea.* The stated vision (as incomplete as our brief statement is) speaks to the context of the church, as it is located in a very ethnically diverse region. Further, the specific mission statements speak to that geographic context in terms of the target ethnic groups. So it appears that Berea's statements stack up fairly well in describing a true missional framework. Are there words and phrases that can be tweaked to even better communicate this framework? Most likely the answer is "yes." But that "tweaking" will best be determined as the congregation works through the process of determining vision and mission, focusing even deeper on its uniqueness.

The Mission(s): Simultaneous or Sequential?

Once the missional framework is established, the question of timing must be addressed. When multiple missions are in play, the organization must determine whether the missions are best carried out at the same time, or if they need to be pursued in a more sequential fashion.

Two issues come to mind when making the determination of whether missions can, or should, be worked simultaneously, or in a sequence. *The first issue is that of resourcing.* The question comes to this: "Does the organization have enough people, systems, financial resources, etc., to effectively work on more than one missional thrust at a time? If so, then how many can be effectively worked?" The organization has to make sure that it doesn't "spread itself too thin," putting itself into a position in which it can't excel for the sake of trying to do too much at one time.

■ **Does the organization have enough people, systems, financial resources, etc., to effectively work on more than one missional thrust at a time?**

The second issue has to do with the *critical path.* The critical path of a project is derived by identifying the steps required to complete a project, along with the anticipated time durations of the steps, as well as the dependencies and interdependencies among those steps. The critical path identifies those steps *most integral to the project,* those that must be completed in sequence, based on dependencies, and on time, for the entire project to be completed in the shortest amount of time.

As it relates to the missional framework and the critical path, two relevant questions are, "Which missional thrusts are independent of the others?" and, "Which missional thrusts are dependent on others, and which ones are they dependent on?" If significant dependencies and interdependencies exist, working missional thrusts simultaneously may not be an option anyway.

In the case of Berea church, addressing the first question of resources shows that Berea is a relatively small church, with less than 100 in attendance and membership. The congregation's very size poses a barrier to working missions simultaneously. Berea will have to deploy its best available people to work a single mission. It doesn't have enough people to work multiple missions at one time.

The second issue in Berea's case, sequencing, should be addressed as well. Adopting this missional framework would be a huge step for Berea, a church that had previously been known as one that had done the same things for years, with little appreciable change. This fact points up that Berea would be better off pursuing one mission at a time, simply because it needs to start slow. The advantage of a sequenced approach for Berea is one of learning. Since all three missions within the framework are so similar, Berea can work one and learn as they go. After completing that first missional thrust, the congregation can move on to the second mission and apply its learnings. Each time it completes a mission and starts a new one, Berea is likely to find that things get smoother each time, and results, then, turn out better each time a mission is accomplished.

Pulling It Together

The vision is all about what *is to be*. The mission is about what *is to be done* to bring the vision to reality. The single comprehensive course of action catalyzes the fulfillment of the vision. An effective mission addresses the question: "What will we do (to get there)?" Depending on the nature of the vision, an organization may focus on *more than one mission* over the life of a vision.

In the congregational context, the *purpose* of the church is the overriding biblical mandate, communicated clearly in the Great Commandment and the Great Commission. This *purpose*, which applies to all churches seeking to be Kingdom-oriented, needs to be distinguished from both the vision and mission of the church, which incorporate the uniqueness of the individual church.

The three primary criteria required for a good mission statement are: (a) an *action orientation*, (b) a *well-defined completion point*, and (c) a *sense of the uniqueness of the congregation*. The innovative congregation will value a meaningful mission that will feature these characteristics, and will thus more effectively mobilize its people.

5

Dimension 3:
Strategic Planning

"How Will It Get Done?"

The joke around our family is that if Dad tries to do anything technical, mechanical, or electrical, the house, cars, yard, etc., stand a good chance of going up in smoke. I am pretty honest about this limitation of mine—not knowing how to do the things that "real men" are supposed to be able to do.

Fortunately, I have been surrounded by guys—and girls—who have an uncanny knack to just know how to do all things technical, mechanical, or electrical. The good news is that I have always been able to get them to help me in this most challenged area of my life. The bad news—I have gotten quite dependent on them and have thus developed little incentive to learn to do this stuff myself.

Learning How

Who are these guys? Let's take, for instance, my dad. I remember writing a story in elementary school titled something like "My Dad Can Fix *Anything.*" I saw him, and still see him, as the perfect example of someone who just *knows how to do things*. I realize now that I have always been intrigued by his ability "to do anything." I also recognize that many kids around me whose dads had similar abilities were not as fascinated by their dads' abilities as I was with my dad's. I think I have figured out that my fascination was driven by my own ineptitude in this area. Even as a kid, I could play ball, sing, swim, etc. But I couldn't fix anything, or put anything together.

I even remember buying model cars that had the fewest pieces to put together. I would even go for the "snap together" cars to avoid all the messy glue!

To compound my chagrin as a nearly nonfunctioning member of the male gender, my brothers both turned out to be a whole lot more like my dad than I did. Then, to top it all, I fell for a young lady whose dad was a builder, and that builder would become my father-in-law! In my early adulthood, I began to realize how easy I had it with all these "handymen" around me!! I should never have to worry about getting anything done—ever again!

After all, knowing how to do this stuff is not *my* strength. But it certainly is a strength of my dad and other guys around me! What was that strength that my dad and brothers had, that I didn't? Well, they may have had more manual dexterity than I did in certain things. But the main thing they had was "know-how." They simply knew *how* to do some of these handyman things that I just wasn't good at. When faced with a problem, such as a blown fuse in a heat pump, a cracked blade on a lawn mower, or checking and changing transmission fluid in a car, they just knew *how* to do it. If they didn't know how to do something, they found out.

The third dimension of planning relates to guys like my dad, my father-in-law, and my brothers. It relates to the know-how when it comes to doing something—in this case, completing the mission(s) of the organization. This third dimension is called *strategic planning*. Unfortunately, while the potential definitions of *vision* and *mission* are certainly all over the map, they are probably not nearly as divergent as the plethora of definitions for *strategic planning*.

What Really Is Strategic Planning?

In many organizational contexts, *strategic planning* is the term used to describe the totality of the planning that goes on. In these contexts, it is more of a generic term that encompasses everything about planning. But is that an accurate depiction? Definitions of the word *strategy* abound. The *American Heritage Dictionary* lends a definite military flair: "The science and art of using all the forces of a nation to execute approved plans as effectively as possible during peace or war. The science and art of military command as applied to the overall planning and conduct of large-scale combat operations."

The dictionary further offers: "A plan of action resulting from strategy or intended to accomplish a specific goal. The art or skill of using stratagems in endeavors such as politics and business."

"How Will We Get It Done?"

Each of the dimensions of planning addresses a key question in moving the organization forward. The vision results from addressing the questions: *"Where are we going? Toward what destination are we heading? What does that destination look like?"* The vision defines the future desired state of the organization. It is all about *what is TO BE.*

■   **Healthy organizational strategies will address the questions: "How will we do it? How will we accomplish the mission?"**

The mission supports the vision and becomes clear from questions such as, *"What will we do—while we are on the way toward that destination?"* The trip toward the visionary destination must be intentional. The trip has an action-orientation as well as a completion point—the destination. In addition, inherent in a healthy mission is the ability to know when that destination has been reached. The mission, then, is about *what is TO BE DONE.*

Healthy organizational strategies will address the questions, *"How will we do it? How will we accomplish the mission?"* It's not enough to know where we are going and what we will do on the way. The organization must have a collective concept of how those things will get done. So, strategies are about *HOW the mission (WHAT IS TO BE DONE) is to be carried out.*

A Focused Plan of Action

For the purposes of understanding the idea of strategy in the context of the *4D* paradigm, our working definition of strategic planning is couched in this simple statement:

While a mission may be defined as a broad course for action designed to facilitate the realization of the vision, a strategy can be viewed as a more focused plan of action designed to facilitate the completion of the mission.

That more focused plan relates to the 'how to." It must be more focused than the mission. Why? Because a strategy defines what must get done to carry out the mission.

Building Blocks

Having "fallen for" a builder's daughter some twenty-seven years ago, I couldn't help but learn to appreciate even more the precision, commitment, and attention to detail required in building a house. My father-in-law was known as a meticulous builder and a master craftsman. He would do everything possible to ensure that every house he built was as sturdy as possible and would last forever. He believed just that—that a house is a permanent structure. He would take whatever time and effort necessary to *do it right!*

Tammy and I had been married less than a year when we moved into the house that my father-in-law built for us. That first year of marriage had been a really good one. At times I was impatient with the time it took for our house to be constructed. This certainly didn't sit well with my new bride, as she fully understood the time frame that it would take her dad to build a quality house that met his personal standards. She knew all along that he was right on schedule. From time to time, she would explain to me how and why her dad used just a limited number of trusted subcontractors and would do so much of the work with his small crew of three—my brother-in-law, a long-time friend/employee, and himself.

One evening as we sat around the dinner table at my father-in-law's house, I made a sarcastic remark about what I thought was a longer-than-necessary time frame for something to be completed on our new house. (That was a big mistake. I was out of line, and there was no need for the comment.) Well—here I was, the consummate "anti-handy man," whose newlywed wife wouldn't even let him hang a picture in our "interim" home, questioning the work of a master craftsman who had plied his trade for nearly forty years.

After realizing what a dumb statement I had made, my father-in-law then proceeded to help me understand the intricacies of building something the right way. He went into a passionate, yet polite and informative, monologue about the elements that must go into a house for it to hold up well for the long haul and about the need to sacrifice time and convenience on the front end for the benefit of time and convenience way into the future.

Needless to say, I "ate crow" that day and was significantly humbled by the whole exchange. But I came away with a much greater understanding of what it takes to build a house the right way. Certainly, I wanted our house to be of the highest quality. Hearing my father-in-law's words opened up a new world for me—not that I was interested in joining his crew. (With my handyman deficiencies, he wouldn't have hired me anyway.) That day I gained a whole new sense of appreciation for all the work that must be done, and all the different elements that must come together, for a quality house to be constructed. I learned about all the building blocks that go into the building process!

Strategies as Building Blocks

In constructing a house, the footing supports the foundation, the foundation supports the framing, and the framing supports the walls. Floor joists support a flooring system—you get the picture... Each of these "support systems" has a dual role. They are each important in their own right as they provide utility within themselves, but they each also support another part of the house. For example, the flooring provides—well, floors, and also provides support for the walls and the rest of the framework.

So it is with strategies. Strategies are the "building blocks" that are necessary for a strong mission. Healthy strategies come to light when the broader mission is broken down into component parts. They will provide support for the accomplishment of the mission and should be constructed in such a way that they foster organizational values and norms and drive behavior that will be favorable and productive within the organization.

Silo Mentality

Many organizations are characterized by a "silo mentality." Organizational consultant and author Pat Lencioni says that "...silos are nothing more than the barriers that exist between departments within an organization, causing people who are supposed to be on the same team to work against one another..."[1] The negative effects of silo mentality are not necessarily exposed when workers in a factory department (or members of a ministry team) go all out in maximizing the success of their department. Rather, the negative effect comes to light when a department focuses so much on meeting its numbers that it makes decisions that hamper the ability of another to make its numbers. Invariably, the result in these situations is that the overall organization misses its numbers.

For example, in a manufacturing company, a production department, acting on its own, may speed up its line and put out product much faster than the manufacturing plan calls for. The department's higher rate of output may make the workers and leaders look good, but what if the accelerated rate of production, unanticipated by the rest of the factory, causes backlogs in the shipping department?

---

[1] Patrick Lencioni, *Silos, Politics and Turf Wars* (SanFrancisco: Jossy-Bass, 2006), 175.

Finished goods pile up, and the company's investment in inventory increases. The production department may have thought it was helping the company as a whole by increasing its rate of output, but it acted in a shortsighted manner. By not coordinating the change with the shipping department, big problems are encountered. The company as a whole suffers, as funds are tied up in product that will sit on the shipping department floor for much longer than called for by the distribution schedule. Late deliveries may result, as well as frustration among the shipping department workers.

A much better result would have occurred if the managers in the production department, once they determined their capabilities for increased production, had coordinated with other departments. Then each of the departments could have adjusted their own capacities to allow for *greater overall factory output*. The company as a whole would then experience greater efficiency, and likely greater profitability.

■   **Strategies within an organization must (a) be carefully developed so that they enable each other to be fulfilled, and (b) be carefully aligned with the mission of the organization.**

Here's the point: Strategies within an organization must (a) be carefully developed so that they enable each other to be fulfilled, and (b) be carefully aligned with the mission of the organization.

Strategic Synergy

Healthy organizational strategies will be in harmony with each other and will move participants—employees, members, etc.—toward action. The innovative congregation, for example, will understand the interdependencies between its ministry teams and will intentionally develop its strategies in such a way that each strategy enables other concurrent strategies to be fulfilled. This *strategic synergy* is a key to the success of an innovative congregation.

The factory example of the production line unilaterally kicking up its output could just as easily show up in a church. Let's say that an evangelism team in ABC Church has worked with other ministry teams, including the growing, worship, and service teams, to develop a complete disciple-making strategy for the upcoming church year (September–August). The team set some evangelistic goals with regard to the number of people in the church anticipated to make professions of faith. Since a natural progression moves a person from conversion into spiritual growth opportunities, the other teams have developed their strategies, set their schedules, and recruited teachers and workers to accommodate these anticipated new converts.

In mid-October, the church team is notified that a very high-energy youth evangelist has a cancellation for a crusade that had been scheduled in the neighboring state. He can come and do a three-night evangelistic crusade for ABC Church in six weeks. The church secretary refers the call to the leader of the evangelism team.

With the quick turnaround, the evangelism team decides it wants to go for it and sends the team leader to the pastor for his concurrence. They agree to move forward with the crusade. After all, this is a great opportunity! The evangelism team works with the evangelist's advance person for the next two weeks, working out logistical details, etc. The next two weeks are spent outside the church, with the evangelism team drumming up promotion all around the area.

A week before the crusade is to begin, the team leader recognizes the need for "follow-up" for those who make professions of faith at the crusade and dispatches one of his team members to meet with the growing team leader to discuss the growing team's role in helping new converts. The growing team leader realizes that with only a week left before the crusade, they have no way to mobilize the needed resources for the crusade. Discouraged, she tries to recruit some folks, but falls well short of the estimated need of fifty counselors.

The crusade takes place, and by the standards of evangelism, is a huge success—135 new converts! The new believers are then referred to the growing team, whose role is to help engage them in studies that will help them learn to follow Christ. The problem is—the growing team can't get to everyone in a timely manner. The end result is that only forty-five of the converts even come to a follow-up meeting the next Sunday after church, and only eighteen of those make follow-up appointments with growing team counselors.

Strategic Synergy in Action

What went wrong with the crusade and the follow-up with new converts? The major problems actually occurred long before the crusade, or the follow-up. First, the decision to do the crusade was made in a vacuum. The opportunity was referred to the evangelism team leader, whose team unilaterally made the decision to go with the crusade. A much better situation would have been for the team leader to bring in the growing team leader to discuss the crusade. Perhaps the decision still would have been made by the evangelism team. But the input of the growing team up front could have ensured at least two things: (1) A better understanding of how the crusade "fit" into the overall mission of the church and the strategies associated with evangelism and growing, and (2) A sense of ownership of the crusade by the growing team.

Had the growing team been brought in much earlier, even with the short notice on the crusade itself, the teams could have planned and coordinated their schedules. Growing could have been preparing its follow-up folks, concurrent with evangelism's efforts to promote and finalize logistics for the event. These efforts would have helped the crusade to come off much more effectively. Growing would have been prepared at the event to engage new converts, and more of them would have received a "post-crusade touch" and an opportunity to get a jump-start on their journey with Christ.

It is critical, then, for organizations to avoid the natural inclination toward silo mentality and to ensure that each of their various strategic initiatives truly support the others.

What Is a Right Strategy?

Perhaps the key question in strategic planning is, "Around what areas of the organization do we strategize?"

Even if the organization's vision and mission is clear, coming up with the appropriate areas of strategic initiatives proves difficult. At least two reasons explain this.

First, many organizations find it difficult to figure out how to build strategy because they contain so many potential activities, requirements, etc., around which strategy could be built. Having so many things needing to be done, the temptation is to jump on as many of them as possible, in hopes of "fixing" as many parts of the organization as possible, or moving the organization forward in various ways.

Second, few organizations—particularly congregations—have a healthy understanding of how to *phase change* into the organization. To avoid overwhelming the members, changes need to be planned for over time. Keeping in mind that strategic initiatives need to be framed so that they can be completed within 1–3 years, this time phasing is critical.

■ Few organizations—particularly congregations, have a healthy understanding of how to phase change into the organization.

Pinpointing the Right Strategies

In developing the appropriate strategic initiatives, at least three key issues must be addressed.

First, *barriers* could prevent the accomplishment of the mission and fulfillment of the vision. Identifying these barriers will be a great place to start with regard to developing strategy. After all, these barriers will have to be overcome. Intentionally focusing energy on the relevant barriers could cause rapid forward movement in the organization.

Second, *opportunities often stand right in front of us* unencumbered by the barriers. One of the easiest things to overlook is an obvious opportunity for success. Often this *low-hanging fruit* represents what we see as having small impact, when in reality the pursuit of this even small success could pave the way for even greater levels of success.

Third, *resources* will be required to tackle these barriers and pursue these opportunities. The resource question is always a difficult one. The vast majority of organizations have a relatively limited pool of resources—human, systemic, and financial—with which to work. An organization must be careful not to bite off more than it can chew by being overly aggressive and taking on too many strategic initiatives at one time. Priority decisions must be made on a continuing basis for resources to be allocated to where they can have the most impact.

■ Barriers, opportunities, and resources are key factors in determining the appropriate strategic initiatives for the organization.

So—*barriers, opportunities, and resources are key factors in determining the appropriate strategic initiatives for the organization.* The organization should devote sufficient time and energy to make sure that these three factors are properly weighed and considered.

The Life Cycle of a Strategy

A well-developed and well-articulated vision can inspire and motivate for a limited time. Generally, the life cycle for the vision is around seven to ten years. Anything that can be realized in less time is probably not really a significant vision, and any initiative that requires a longer time for fulfillment will likely lose momentum, simply because those people pursuing it will become tired of it, and energy will wane.

> ■ **The organization needs to help the members see continued successes, so as to generate and sustain positive momentum.**

A solid and relevant mission, as it supports the realization of the vision, and with an action orientation and a completion point, probably needs to be accomplished within a three-to-five-year time frame. The idea with a mission is that the organization needs to help the members see continued successes, so as to generate and sustain positive momentum. This momentum will inspire organizational members to continue pressing forward toward the mission's accomplishment and the realization of the vision.

Healthy strategies, however, should be geared toward successful fulfillment over a one-to-three-year time span. Again, a healthy strategy will support the accomplishment of the mission. Also, healthy strategies will not conflict with, but rather will complement, other strategies geared toward accomplishing the mission. Healthy strategies are indeed building blocks for the organization's mission. In addition, strategic initiatives should be significant enough to stimulate behavioral change in the organization. Any initiative that can be accomplished in less than one year will likely not be far-reaching enough to effect that behavioral change.

Behavioral Change

Healthy organizational planning should be developed with organizational behavior in mind. Strategies should also be aligned with the organization's values. When looking inside a successful organization, one will usually (if not always) discover a *strong sense of shared values* among the members. A healthy organization will exude healthy shared values. Unfortunately, in an unhealthy organization, the opposite will likely be true.

Strategic planning is the dimension at which the organization can best help drive behavioral change. *A by-product of a clear vision, an action-oriented mission, and healthy strategies will always be positive behavioral change.* A clear vision defines a future state—a new and improved state—for the organization. The fulfillment of that vision will naturally require people to do things differently than they have in the past, simply because the vision defines a destination that looks different from the place where the organization currently finds itself. This positive behavioral shift must intensify with time, so that progress toward the vision will be sustained.

■ A by-product of a clear vision, an action-oriented mission, and healthy strategies will always be positive behavioral change.

This positive behavioral change, to be permanent, must also be sustainable long after the vision has been realized. Otherwise, the organization will likely suffer a relapse, and regress into a state of mediocrity. The key, then, is to help organizational members develop new habits that will ultimately drive their behavior beyond the foreseeable future.

■ With each sequential dimension of planning —vision, mission, and then strategy— there is greater potential for influencing the behavior of the organizational members.

With each sequential dimension of planning—vision, mission, and then strategy—the potential for influencing the behavior of the organizational members increases. Because strategy is a little more *nuts and bolts,* more people can understand it than can understand vision and mission. For this reason, it is good for strategies to be framed in such a way that they promote the behavioral change that the organization needs.

What Do We Measure?

A strategy is not complete without the incorporation of the appropriate metrics that will help measure progress toward the completion of the strategic initiative. Again, the organization's members need to know what success looks like, and they need to know when they have been successful. Continued success provides motivation for these members. An appropriate metric will measure both progress toward that success and will define the point at which success has been achieved.

In many organizations, the focus is on purely objective metrics, such as finances, numbers of people, schedules, facilities, etc. Other trends, such as professional development, or personal and spiritual growth, are not as quantifiable. Progress in areas such as these are, by nature, more subjective, and thus more difficult to measure. Greater care must be taken to determine how to best measure progress toward completion of the strategic initiative. The more subjective that which requires measurement, the more time and energy will be required to develop the metric. Whatever the measure, the strategy development is not complete until the metric is clearly defined, and in place, to measure progress.

Strategic Planning with Berea Church

Let's go back to our example of "semi-fictional" Berea Church from the previous chapter. Berea's vision (in a simplified statement) incorporates the idea of becoming the *"leading multicultural ministry in our region of the state."*

Within the context of that vision, Berea would adopt three distinct missions that would support the replication of that vision. Let's focus on one of them:

> To build a substantial population of Hispanics into the Berea church family.

Berea's other missions in support of this vision are similar, except that they relate to the other prominent ethnic groups. However, with the Hispanic community being the fastest-growing ethnicity in the region, the church chooses to pursue this initiative first. To accomplish the mission, Berea must develop healthy strategies that will further the mission *and* drive positive behavioral change. The church should also take a good hard look to see where barriers may stand, and where areas of opportunity are apparent. Finally, the church must consider the level of resources at its disposal.

Berea Church gives careful consideration of the mission and the potential strategies that support the mission. The church enlists Hispanic church consultants at the denominational level to assist in the research and decision-making process. Ultimately, the leaders at Berea decide on three strategic initiatives in reaching out to the Hispanics in this diverse county.

Strategic Initiative 1: Education of the current Berea congregation concerning the indigenous culture of Hispanics living in the region.

- *Barrier:* The Berea folks are *not very knowledgeable of the Hispanics* in the area. A survey taken by the church members pointed up that only about 20 percent of the Berea regulars even know a Hispanic family, much less the cultural nuances that characterize their lives. A great deal of learning will have to take place.
- *Opportunity:* Because the congregation at Berea *has been on board with the vision and mission of the church,* the majority of members claim that they are ready to learn.
- *Resources:* Because of the all-encompassing nature of this strategic initiative, the church will encourage *all regular members*

of the congregation to participate at some level of learning about the other cultures in the region.

- *Metric:* Intense learning opportunities would be made available to the congregation over a *one-year period, with the goal of two thirds of active membership participating* in the educational process.

Strategic Initiative 2: An intentional approach to ministering to Hispanics in the region. Berea's folks would pull together demographic information and go out into the community to be among the Hispanics and to serve their needs.

- *Barrier:* The Berea congregation at this point knows very little about the Hispanic culture and of the specific needs of the Hispanics in their region. They would take their time in building relationships within the Hispanic community and would avoid "pushing" their church on the folks.
- *Opportunity:* Effectively penetrating the Hispanic culture would build an atmosphere of openness with the Hispanics, making them more comfortable with the idea of coming to Berea. The major target would be English-speaking Hispanics, with a secondary goal of helping them assimilate into American culture. Besides, at this point, the church can only afford to pay expenses for a Hispanic lay pastor.
- *Resources:* All regular members who participated significantly in learning opportunities will be encouraged to participate in this next initiative. This initiative will be sequential, beginning after the completion of strategic initiative 1.
- *Metric:* This initiative is planned to span a period of eighteen months, with a twofold goal:
    1. Three quarters of those regular members who participated in the learning will "go out" into the Hispanic culture beyond the walls of the church to serve Hispanics.
    2. Ten Hispanic family units will have attended Berea at the end of the period.

Strategic Initiative 3: Assimilation of the Hispanic families into the life of the church.

- *Barrier:* Berea's leaders know this may be the toughest leg of the mission. Living in their own culture in their own unique community, Berea leaders know it will be tough for area Hispanics to integrate into a previously all-Caucasian church. The leaders admit that they really don't know what this *assimilation* will look like and that there may be a period of "trial and error" before they can figure out what works for the Hispanic community.

- *Opportunity:* Berea's leaders are willing to adjust the church's worship style to appeal more to the potential newcomers. Also, they recognize that a separate Hispanic mission church, on the Berea campus, may be the best way for the initiative to be successful.
- *Resources:* Many of the folks who have worked to this point on the issue of the assimilation of the Hispanics will continue on. However, some will be encouraged to move to the second missional thrust of assimilating African Americans into the church, preparing the church for that particular focus.
- *Metric:* Leaders decided to give this assimilation phase a minimum of one year, with a goal of twelve Hispanic families being integrated into the life of the church as a whole.

For each of these three strategic initiatives, Berea Church would write out a more specific plan. Their idea is that when this three-and-a-half-year period is complete, church members will evidence significant behavioral shift, with the most obvious change being a new outward focus. Also, Berea's leaders expect that some of the folks who have worked this project will continue working with the Hispanic community, while others will move on to work in Berea's next missional objective, using a similar approach in reaching the African American community.

Assessing Berea's Strategic Plans

How does Berea Church's strategic plan development stack up against the criteria set forth in this chapter?

Strategic Synergy

Each of the three strategic initiatives seem to support the others. The three initiatives focus on education of the Berea folks, penetration into the Hispanic community, and assimilation of Hispanics into the life of Berea Church. These particular initiatives need to be worked sequentially. With sequential strategies, the potential success of each strategic initiative is dependent upon the success of the previous initiatives. In this way, the initiatives may be viewed as building blocks. For example, penetration into the Hispanic community by Berea Church will not be successful without an understanding of the Hispanic culture, which comes with the first strategic initiative. Likewise, assimilation of Hispanics into Berea church will never occur without successful completion of the second initiative—the penetration into the Hispanic community through serving opportunities.

■   **With sequential strategies, the potential success of each strategic initiative is dependent upon the success of the previous initiatives.**

Barriers, Opportunities, and Resources

The major barrier for the Berea Church members seems to be a lack of knowledge about the Hispanic culture in their geographic region. The initial strategy of education will help to overcome that barrier and will allow them to move more freely and comfortably in and out of the Hispanic culture. Other barriers will likely come into play as the church moves forward. For example, another major barrier is the historic tendency of the church to be inward-focused. Only time will tell whether the enthusiasm surrounding this vision and mission will sustain or wane.

The greatest *opportunity*, perhaps, is the fact that the diversity in the region is growing at such a rapid rate. Berea could perhaps be only marginally effective in regard to this mission and could very possibly still see ten Hispanic families "stick" with the church.

Another great opportunity seems to loom in *the church members' realization that they need to change.* Their inward-focus of the past has given way to discontent with the status quo. That the church is asking questions about the diverse demographic of its region is encouraging.

As a small church, the availability of *resources*, particularly human, will be at a premium. However, it does appear that this three-pronged "strategic set" supports nicely where the church is today. That the three strategies are, in effect, sequential in nature will allow the church to use the same people in each initiative. Besides, those who are educated in the cultural nuances will need to be the ones who go into the community. For assimilation to be effective, those who go into the community, building relationships through serving the needs of the community, should be the ones the Hispanics encounter as they come to Berea's campus.

The Life Cycle/Behavioral Change

The timing of Berea's mission—becoming the *"leading multicultural ministry in our region of the state"*—is set for a three-and-a-half-year period. The church is focusing on (a) education of it own people for the first year, (b) moving out into the Hispanic community through service projects for the next eighteen months, and then, (c) ,for the next year, assimilating into the life of the Berea church family those Hispanics who have begun coming to the Berea campus.

Each of the three strategies are geared toward a greater degree of behavioral change. The church will certainly face significant challenges with each strategic initiative. But these challenges should work to change hearts, attitudes, and actions of those within the church toward the Hispanics. The ultimate result will be a church that is very diverse, reflecting the demographic of the church's environment.

Metrics

The effectiveness of Berea's strategic initiatives will have to be measured. The twelve-month education initiative has a goal of having two thirds of the current church members going through the process. It is an aggressive proposition for any church to attempt to engage that high a proportion of its population in just about anything. In addition, the church will need to find a way to gauge the quality of the education and training. This will be a bit more subjective and may not be obvious until the second initiative—moving into the Hispanic community—has begun.

The situation is similar for the second and third strategic initiatives as well. Measurements of people affected by the initiatives may be relatively simple. But at the same time Berea will need to determine how to assess the quality of its work. This will not be simple.

Pulling It Together

While a mission may be defined as a *broad course for action,* a strategy can be viewed as a *more focused plan of action.* Strategies are the "building blocks" that come to light when the broader mission is broken down into component parts.

Healthy organizational strategies will address the questions, "How will we do it? How will we accomplish the mission?" Each of the strategies will be synergistic with all the others and will move participants—employees, members, etc.—toward action. This *strategic synergy* is key to the success of an innovative congregation.

A vision can be viewed with a long-term (seven to ten years) perspective, while a mission can be viewed with an intermediate (three to five years) to long-term perspective. Healthy strategies are usually geared toward successful fulfillment over a one to three-year time span. The longer the duration of the strategic initiative, the greater chance that it will generate the behavioral shifts the organization desires.

Significant factors in determining the right strategic initiatives for the organization are *barriers, opportunities, and resources.* Three key questions must be asked:

1. "What barriers are keeping us from accomplishing the mission and fulfilling the vision?"
2. "What opportunities are right there and are unencumbered by those barriers?"
3. "What is our level of resources—human, financial, and systemic—and how will our strategic initiatives require us to allocate these resources to bring about the desired changes?"

An organization may effectively handle multiple concurrent strategies, depending on the strength of its resources. Again, as with mission, the question of *sequential or simultaneous* will come into play.

Finally, the organization must understand that momentum among its members is most often created by successes. The organization's leaders must develop the strategic initiatives in such a way that (a) the members know what success looks like, (b) members know when success has been achieved, and (c) progress toward that success is constantly measured. Therefore, it is critical that the proper metrics are developed to track that progress.

6

Dimension 4:
Tactical Planning

"Who Will Do It, and When?"

The day was really good, actually. Our church had been going through the proverbial "summer doldrums"—you know, with church families traveling and taking part in fun summer activities. We had pretty much focused on making our weekend celebrations the best they could be. After all, with peoples' attention diverted so much during the summer, we did not have a lot of other things we could do.

A Good Day's Activities

Other things did go on. As the lead pastor of a multi-staff medium-sized church, I had grown accustomed to not knowing everything—or even most of the things—that were going on in our church. As a matter of fact, I had come to the point over the previous years that whenever I was asked about something going on in one of our ministry areas, I would enjoy saying, "I don't know about that. As a matter of fact, I don't know about a lot of things that are going on in the church." (Often the looks I got in return indicated the questioner's disbelief that I, as the lead pastor, did not, in fact, know *everything* that was going on!)

On this day—a good day, actually—a lot was going on—much of which I didn't know much about. (Again—no surprise there!) That day our folks were preparing and serving breakfast at the local homeless shelter. Later in the day, our children's ministry team, partnering with our local missions team, had planned a major ministry event in a local low-income housing apartment complex. The children's team brought their full-blown drama and musical ministry to the local complex clubhouse. That evening our adult music team played at an outreach event for a local biker ministry. I had returned from a trip the night before just so I could take in at least a couple of these events.

While all of these events turned out really well, the one that stood out to me the most was the afternoon at the apartment complex. When I arrived that afternoon, I noticed something strange: while a large number of residents were there from the apartment complex, even more folks from our church were present!

During the program, our children's team performed very well. As our folks served dinner to anyone and every one of the residents that wanted to come out, I got connected with the complex's director, who doubled as a staff member at her church. Ramona is a lady of vision—one who works tirelessly to make the complex a better place for the residents, and for the town in general. Her passion is built around serving, and in engaging her church and others to join her there. That afternoon, Ramona reminded me once again just how little I knew about what was going on at our church!

Ramona told me over and over just how she appreciated all our folks had done for her and the residents—not just that day, but over the course of the previous months and even couple of years. It seems that our folks had been building relationships that go well beneath the surface. Ramona even went so far to tell me about the frustrations they had had with many ministries that had come in and made commitments to the complex. These ministries stayed a while, doing their programs and then leaving. But they never built any relationships "beneath the surface" with the residents. Ultimately, they pulled out and never came back—often without even informing Ramona.

Well, tears nearly came to my eyes as Ramona told me how different it had been with our church—and I didn't even know this stuff had been going on! She told me of the many times during the week when our people would come by and encourage her, or just talk to the residents to see what they needed. She told me about the guys in our church who would come by after a full day of work to work on the playground, or the lawns in front of the buildings. She was so impressed that none of these people wanted any recognition for any of this. Needless to say, this conversation was fairly lengthy—but I certainly enjoyed hearing it!

Whom Do You Thank?

Ramona then moved on to brag about our folks for the work that was going on that particular day. Having heard all this, I was determined to thank all of our folks for all the good work they had done, and were doing, in partnership with the complex. As soon as I broke away, I found Chuck, our missions pastor, a gifted visionary and strategist in his own right, and thanked him. His reply: "Don't thank me. I didn't do anything in pulling this together. I didn't know much about it. I just showed up!"

"Hmmm...," I thought. "Chuck sounds a lot like me. He doesn't know what's going on either! Glad there's somebody else!"

He told me that some of the team members came up with the idea and ran with it. Said I should to go see Karen and thank her. She had put it all together. So I went to find Karen, who serves as the missions director within our children's ministry. As I thanked her, she gave me a puzzled look and said she really did nothing, other than sending a few e-mails about the event. She told me that from those e-mails, people started catching on. Before she knew it, everything was in place!

I began to understand how one of my heroes, Coach Jim Valvano, felt after the 1983 N.C. State NCAA Championship Game victory over Houston, running around the court, in the midst of bedlam, looking for someone to hug!

So I went around just saying, "Thanks," to everyone I could find—without elaboration.

Get Out of the Doers' Way

A number of lessons can be learned from my day with our missions and children's teams at the apartment complex. One stands out above the rest:

> The best thing an organization can do for its "doers" is to give them a little direction and get out of their way!

I discovered again the value of people who are committed to a cause. When they are working in an area of passion, motivation doesn't have to be manufactured. More on that later.

Thinking a bit more that night as I was sitting in our music team's concert at the biker outreach ministry, I tried to figure out the reasons why we—and churches in general—don't see this type of thing from our volunteers on a more regular basis. My best guess came down to two main reasons:

1. Leaders often don't do a very good job of translating the organization's vision, mission, and strategies into grassroots action steps that can bring traction in moving the organization forward.

2. We can devalue our best people by not helping them find opportunities to work in their "sweet spot." In describing the characteristics of companies that have made the transition to greatness, Jim Collins explains:

> The executives who ignited the transformations from good to great did not first figure out where to drive the bus and then get people to take it there. No, they first got the right people on the bus (and the wrong people off the bus) and figured out where to drive it. They said, in essence, "Look, I don't really know where we should take this bus. But I know this much: If we get the right people on the bus, the right people in the right seats, and the wrong people off the bus, then we'll figure out how to take it someplace great.[1]

■ **We tend to try to make the people fit the organization, instead of looking for the right people, and "tweaking" the organization and the "way we do business" to fit the people.**

In other words, we tend to try to make the people fit the organization, instead of looking for the right people and "tweaking" the organization and the "way we do business" to fit the people we have on board.

Dreamers to Doers

How can we leverage the strengths of the doers to ensure that the organization reaches maximum results? We can do a number of things.

First, let's make sure we understand the nature of the "doer" as well as that of the other two types of people we will generally find in an organization.

The "dreamer" is, in the simplest sense, a visionary. We discussed vision and visionaries in chapter 3. Most likely, you will have visionaries in the organization. The real issue is whether the organization will allow them to manifest that visionary tendency.

---

[1]Jim Collins, *Good to Great* (New York: HarperCollins, 2001), 41.

Many organizational structures are based almost solely on "position." Such organizations will promote people on the basis of competency—usually in areas of technical skills—without taking into account the perspective with which the individual views his or her job. If the organization can find a way to match the dreamer with a role in which the tendency to dream can be utilized, then the organization has the potential to be much more focused and productive. The question then becomes whether or not the dream, or vision, can be communicated effectively enough so that others in the organization can work together in such a way that the vision has a good chance of being fulfilled.

■ **Vision alone will likely frustrate doers, while vision with a roadmap will motivate doers.**

Vision without an accompanying direction to bring the vision to fulfillment will frustrate those nonvisionary thinkers in the organization. In other words, the doers—the "get it done" folks—need the vision stated in such a way that they can grasp it, and own it. The vision, as we defined it, is a picture of a future destination, while the mission and strategies associated with that vision provide the direction and constitute the roadmap. When the members of an organization have a sense of the organization's direction, and understand that direction, they will be more likely to contribute in moving the organization forward toward that destination. The bottom line: Vision alone will likely frustrate doers, while vision with a roadmap will motivate doers. This is where the *developers* come in.

The Middlemen: Dreamers to Developers to Doers

Even in organizations with a healthy quotient of dreamers and the freedom to dream, a big issue remains. Are visionary dreams communicated to those who have to carry out the work in such a way that they can understand them? The message of the vision, then, needs to be translated from the visionaries to the doers, where the work gets done.

Organizations need translators to help dreamers and doers understand each other. I like to refer to these translators as "developers." The developers are those who work between the dreamers and the doers, helping to shift the dream, or vision, from the realm of the dreamer (who flies at perhaps a 30,000 feet cruising altitude) into the realm of the doer (who may fly at 5,000 to 10,000 feet), where things can actually get done!

Developers, in effect, "process" the vision of the dreamer, perhaps talking at length with the dreamer, rolling the vision over and over again in their minds. They develop (so the term "developer") plans that are clearer to those in the organization who will be charged with fulfilling the vision. For the developer, the vision is the equivalent of the "raw materials" in a manufacturing process. The missional and strategic plans that come from the work of the developer become the "finished product" ready to pass on to the doers.

Tactical Planning: "What Is It?"

In an innovative organization characterized by healthy planning, the strategic plans passed on by the developers to the doers make way for what happens in the fourth dimension of planning— tactical planning. The organization gains real traction ultimately in the day-to-day operations. Tactical planning is the dimension in which the doers in an organization typically become most engaged. The organization's leadership must see that the doers have what they need to get their job done. Tactical planning is actually less about planning and more about execution, within the context of a strategic plan. After all, all the planning in the world will go for naught if it is not carried out with effectiveness and efficiency.

The tactical dimension of planning reveals the quality of the planning in the three preceding dimensions. Quality work in the visionary, missional, and strategic dimensions for an organization will often lead to a smooth tactical planning process, and, ultimately, to the plans actually being fulfilled. Conversely, haphazard work at these three levels will hamper the work at the tactical level.

■ **It is ultimately in the day-to-day operations that the organization gains real traction.**

The *American Heritage Dictionary* carries some interesting definitions of the word *tactics*:

1a) The military science that deals with securing objectives set by strategy, especially the technique of deploying and directing troops, ships, and aircraft in effective maneuvers against an enemy: Tactics is a required course at all military academies.

1b) Maneuvers used against an enemy: Guerrilla tactics were employed during most of the war.

2) A procedure or set of maneuvers engaged in to achieve an end, an aim, or a goal.

Tactical planning, by name, is indeed used most frequently in the realm of military operations. However, tactical planning is necessary for all operations in any realm or discipline. Many organizations miss this—particularly congregations.

We have already discussed the common problem of *a lack of corporate language around planning*. As a result, we hear phrases like strategic planning, long-range planning, visioning, etc., used almost interchangeably. Because so much of this terminology does relate to higher-level planning (30,000 feet altitude kind of stuff), little energy and focus is left by the time the congregation gets to the point of doing the tactical, day-to-day planning that ultimately makes it all happen. In many congregations this results in the planning process never being completed, since the tactical dimension is not addressed. As a result, plans that may be based on really good ideas may never become reality.

The real problem is: the congregation never really understood the multiple dimensions of planning and how to navigate effectively through them.

A Natural Flow

Perhaps the most important part of the dictionary definition is the very first part, which refers to tactics: *"....deals with securing objectives set by strategy."* The key point is that tactics will flow naturally from a strategic plan. In other words, a well-developed strategic plan will make the tactical steps somewhat obvious.

Each planning dimension in the *4D* paradigm addresses unique questions:

- **Visionary Planning:** "Where are we going? What does it look like?"
- **Missional Planning:** "What will we do while we are moving toward our destination?"
- **Strategic Planning:** "How will we do what we need to do while moving toward our destination?"
- **Tactical Planning:** "When will they get it done?" "Who will do what needs to be done?"

Tactical planning moves the organization into the realm of execution. The tactical dimension of planning defines the day-to-day operations of the organization, identifies and holds accountable those responsible for the related tasks and actions, and specifies the timing for the accomplishment of those tasks and actions.

■ The tactical dimension of planning addresses and defines the day-to-day operations of the organization, identifies and holds accountable those responsible for the related tasks and actions, and specifies the timing for the accomplishment of those tasks and actions.

The Tactical Planning Horizon

The *tactical horizon* will be more short-term, most likely less than one year. A tactical plan may be broken down even further, into daily or weekly components. For example, let's assume that the vast majority of tactical operations within a congregation take place on Sunday mornings. Each Sunday, guests and members alike are welcomed, children are taught and cared for, teens are likely to gather for their own worship experience. Also, sermon, music, media, and drama may all be used to get across what is hopefully a relevant and impacting message.

Let's assume further that the congregation believes that 90 percent of its influence on its attendees comes from Sunday morning activities. Therefore, great emphasis is placed on the *Sunday morning experience*, and great energy goes into making each of these experiences the best it can be. The tactical plans for this congregation, then, will likely center on the Sunday morning experience. The planning horizon for this church is weekly, resulting in fifty-two planning tactical cycles in a year.

Potential Pitfalls to Watch Out For

Real dangers arise in the tactical dimension of planning. Even if the organization has a clear corporate language around the idea of planning and a clear understanding of the nature of tactical planning, potential land mines must be avoided. Congregations are notorious for planning new things and then not following through with them. Here are just a few of those dangers:

- **Loss of momentum**—A healthy planning process can require lots of time, energy, and resources. Any organization going through such a process must make a major commitment to do whatever is required to complete the process. A number of "momentum-killers" can stall the process.

  ~ *Fatigue*—Leaders can become tired in working the first two or three planning dimensions. They have less energy to give, perhaps, as time goes on in the process. As a result, in the tactical dimension, where finishing the job is so critical, the work may never be completed.

~ *The distraction of the day-to-day*—It is often difficult to balance the time and energy required for regular daily operations and that required for a planning process. Organizational leaders are often reluctant to offload enough day-to-day responsibilities for a planning participant to spend sufficient time and energy to do an adequate job in the planning process.

~ *The tyranny of the urgent*—So often planning processes, focused on long-term health and growth, fall victim to daily emergencies that impact more short-term issues and measures. When these emergencies occur, the planning process often stops, and participants are pulled to work those emergencies.

- **Fumbled handoffs**—Passing the ball from one dimension to the next can be hazardous. Great care needs to be taken in every interchange between those involved in each of the planning dimensions in an organization. For example, visionaries must communicate well with missional thinkers, who must in turn ensure that the strategists have clarity on visionary and missional thrusts. Likewise, strategists must do a very good job in referring and clarifying strategic plans to doers. Miscommunication in any of these interchanges can lead to misalignment between the dimensions.

- **Over-confidence**—The assumption may be that the day-to-day stuff will also go well simply because the planning process has gone well. Not true! This is where execution must be regularly assessed and acted upon.

- **"Back to Egypt"**—Turning new ways of doing things into habits takes discipline. The work associated with implementing new plans, processes, etc., is often quite difficult. Developing new habits takes effort! Often workers, on realizing this, will begin to revert to the way things used to be done. There, things are comfortable and cause less uncertainty.

Tactical Planning and the Doer

An organization must be careful to remember that it likely has more folks who identify with the tactical dimension of planning (doers) than with any of the other dimensions (visionary/dreamers, missional thinkers/developers and strategists/developers). Often in the typical organization, those who are doers are positioned somewhere near the lower layers of the organizational hierarchy—simply because of their diligence and technical competence. Therefore, the organization must take great care to make sure these folks stay highly motivated. The organization must maintain high levels of communication between leadership and those doers functioning at operational levels. In short, no organization succeeds without effective and efficient doers!

■ **An organization must be careful to remember that it likely has more folks who identify with the tactical dimension of planning (doers) than with any of the other dimensions.**

In perhaps no other organization is the importance of the doer evidenced more than in the church. The local church, for the most part, is a volunteer organization that doesn't have the luxury of motivating and holding accountable its workers through a paycheck. Rather, it must rely on its people—mainly volunteers—to get things done.

The innovative congregation will value its *doers* just as much, if not more, than its *dreamers* and will find ways to reward those doers. An individual church often has no more than ten minutes to make an impression on the first-time guests. Within ten minutes of stepping foot on campus, the church's guests decide whether or not they will return. In most churches, this ten minutes is up long before the guests have heard the pastor teach, seen the drama team act, and in many cases it is before they have even seen and heard the music.

The church's doers "touch" these attenders in those first ten minutes and ultimately make the impressions that determine whether the visitors come back. These doers include the following:

- the volunteers who mow the grass and keep the facilities attractive;
- the greeters in the parking lot;
- the ushers at the door who welcome guests and hand them bulletins;
- the nursery workers and children's workers who greet the young mothers at the nursery, hold their infants, watch their toddlers, and teach their children while the moms and dads participate in the adult worship service.

Rick Warren, pastor of Saddleback Church, writes on creating an atmosphere of acceptance:

Plants need the right climate to grow and so do churches.
The right climate for church growth is an atmosphere
of acceptance and love. Growing churches love; loving
churches grow. It seems obvious, but it is often overlooked:
For your church to grow you must be nice to people when
they show up!

In the survey of the unchurched that I took prior to
beginning Saddleback, the second most common complaint I
discovered was "Church members are unfriendly to visitors.
We feel we don't fit. Long before the pastor preaches, the
visitors are already deciding whether they will come back.
They are asking themselves, "Do I feel welcome here?"[2]

How important are the doers in a congregation? A good gauge
of their effectiveness will be the opinions of first-time guests in the
church!

Finding the Best Doers

> ■   **Leaders must resist the temptation of lumping everybody else
> (who doesn't fit into the previous three dimensions of planning)
> into the category of doers.**

The doers in an organization must be carefully selected. Leaders
must resist the temptation of lumping everybody else (who doesn't
fit into the previous three dimensions of planning), into the category
of doers. You need to consider a number of critical things in finding
the best doers. Here are just a few:

- **Focus** is the ability to keep one's attention fixed on an individual, a situation, etc., and not allow peripheral "goings
  on" to become distractions. Nothing is more annoying than a
  church greeter engaging a first-time guest in conversation, and
  then breaking away in the middle of it to speak to a friend.
- **Responsibility** is the tendency to follow through and to make
  sure the job is finished. The responsible teen ministry worker
  who tells the middle school student he will call him and take
  him for a milk shake after school will not leave the student
  hanging. He will follow through!
- **Interpersonal Skills** are so critical. So often the doers are the
  ones who come closest to the customer—i.e., in the church

sense, the attender. Church greeters can be really sincere, but without a good personality, they are not likely to influence people to return to your church.

- **A specialty or specialties** should be carefully utilized. Doers will usually be willing to leverage that specialty in the service of the church for the benefit of others. The doer will usually interact with other people in the context of performing in the realm of that specialty. For example, a nursery worker with experience as a mother, in nurturing children, will likely be a much more valuable nursery worker than one without such experience. Similarly, the experienced nursery worker will not function so well if placed in a position outside her or his specialty.

- **Initiative** is the tendency for one to be a self-starter. Folks with initiative seem to have the inward drive to "just do it." Not only do they know when something needs to be done, but they seem to know what to do! This seems to be a very rare quality these days. One of the most frustrating things for me, in our church on Sunday morning, is to have to whisper in the ear of a first impressions team member, reminding him or her to go speak to a first-time guest or relative newcomer. On the other hand, a number of the team members have initiative and do not need such prodding. Those with initiative are most often reliable, capable, and can see where their roles fit into the big picture of the organization.

Motivating the Doers

The natural distinctions between dreamer and doer can easily frustrate the doer. But the work of the developer is important in motivating the doer to help move the organization forward.

Motivating the doer is probably not very complicated. Those folks who like to just get the job done probably need three key things from the organization's leadership.

■ **Doers need to see enough of the big picture in order for them to get it.**

First, they need to see enough of the *big picture* for them to *get it*. Typically, missional and strategic thinkers need to see a fairly significant portion of the overall vision to be motivated. They are wrapped up in the "whys" and "hows" of the vision. Doers, on the other hand, are often self-motivated individuals whose personal satisfaction with a specific job well done is often enough to keep them going. Often, the doer's own sense of excellence is enough. He or she may not need to see a big portion of the overall vision.

> ■ **Doers are often self-motivated individuals whose personal satisfaction with a specific job well done is often enough to keep them going.**

Second, while the doers may not need to see the whole vision to be motivated, they will likely want to see enough of it to understand where they *fit in* within the context of the organization. Fit is important with doers. I was reminded of this on the afternoon we spent at the apartment complex. The folks there were generally not content to mingle with their teammates and the residents. They were looking for something to do. Just sitting around was not an option for them. They were drawn to the event because they were aware that they had a "fit," and they wanted to find it and get moving within that fit.

Third, the organization's leadership must not only help the doers to see enough of the big picture to know where they will fit in. The organization must assume responsibility for helping the doers understand how they can be the most *productive* in that fit. Leveraging the talents and strengths of the doers will be key to the overall success of the organization. However, that is easier said than done. Marcus Buckingham, referring to research he has done with Gallup, states:

> Globally, only 20% of employees working in the large organizations we surveyed feel that their strengths are in play every day. Most bizarre of all, the longer an employee stays with an organization and the higher he climbs the traditional career ladder, the less likely he is to strongly agree that he is playing to his strengths...
>
> This discovery actually represents a tremendous opportunity for great organizations. To spur high-margin growth and thereby increase their value, great organizations need only focus inward to find the wealth of unrealized capacity that resides in every single employee.[3]

> ■ **Leveraging the talents and strengths of the doer will be key to the overall success of the organization.**

---

[3]Marcus Buckingham and Donald O. Clifton, *Now Discover Your Strengths* (New York: The Free Press, 2001), 6.

Doers don't have to know everything about the organization. Nor do they have to see the whole big picture. They have to know just enough to see how they fit in, how their part really matters, how they can best be productive, and thus be helpful in moving the organization forward.

Because doers are often not "big picture" people by nature, they don't generally need to see the organization's vision. Thus their idea of success may not be tied to the success of the overall organization. Their sense of fulfillment may be tied to their success at their own personal level. The downside of this perspective is that doers can be very susceptible to the "silo mentality" we previously discussed. They may get so focused on their own jobs that they ignore opportunities to work across departmental lines to help the organization be more successful.

In the innovative organization, "doers" will likely have ample opportunity to move around into different roles, stay fresh, and have great impact. The very nature of an innovative organization, with its constant transition and adaptation, will likely encourage such movement in the interest of meeting the needs of an ever-changing environment.

Pulling It Together

Vision in an organization is of little value if it cannot be replicated. Often the doers are the ones in the organization who ultimately carry out the functions that most readily define the organization. However, often a wide communication gap separates the dreamers (the visionaries) and the doers. The developers (missional thinkers and strategic thinkers) are typically those who translate between the dreamers and the doers. They serve as the communication "middlemen" in the organization.

The fourth dimension of planning, tactical planning, deals with the role of the doer in the organization. Tactical planning involves the recognition that it is ultimately in the day-to-day operations that the organization gains real traction. Tactical planning is actually less about planning and more about getting things done within the context of a strategic plan.

A good tactical plan addresses the dual questions of, "Who will do it?" and, "When will they get it done?" It defines the day-to-day operations of the organization and those responsible for the related tasks and actions. At the tactical level, the planning horizon will be more short-term, most likely less than one year, often weekly and even daily.

Organizational leaders must be careful of the pitfalls associated with poor or nonexistent tactical planning. Primary considerations include the need to make sure that the overall planning process does not suffer from a lack of momentum, and that effective handoffs occur between individuals focusing on differing dimensions of planning.

The innovative congregation values its *doers* just as much as its *dreamers*. The doers are often the ones "on the line." They are typically the ones who "touch" the customers and ultimately make the impressions that determine whether customers stick.

The doers in an organization must be carefully selected. The most effective doers will have qualities such as focus, responsibility, good interpersonal skills, and initiative. Often, the best doers in an organization just seem to "know what to do."

Afterword: Confidence at Creekside

The planning retreat for Creekside Community Church turned out fairly well. That's amazing because Jason Conner's sense of dread about the upcoming planning retreat had almost brought him to a state of paralysis. Not knowing what to do, five days before the retreat, he had just about decided to postpone it. He would simply reschedule it for about six months out and do his homework in the meantime, so he could be prepared.

However, that very evening as he was writing a letter to be sent to all who had committed to participate in the retreat, Jason received a call from Bill Henley, one of the Creekside "retreaters," who happened to serve as a CEO at a middle-sized manufacturing company headquartered in a neighboring town. Bill asked Jason what he was planning for the retreat. Sheepishly, Jason confessed his struggles of the past few weeks leading up to the retreat, the fact that he had no plans for the retreat, and that he was just writing the letter to postpone the event.

After hearing Jason's frustrations, Bill then asked Jason if he could offer his help for the retreat. If Jason were willing to go forward, then Bill would facilitate the event, with the goal of helping Creekside begin the development of a comprehensive plan to help the congregation move forward. Bill's confidence won Jason over. Jason decided to move ahead with the retreat, and to let Bill lead the event.

The decision turned out to be a good one. Bill demonstrated a great command of the event and displayed a unique ability to engage all the folks who attended the retreat in the discussion. Jason left the retreat feeling very good, since it looked like the group—and the church—would be moving forward.

Bill led the group in outlining a process by which over the next few months, the team would lead the church in

- firming up the vision that Jason had been talking about during the past few months.
- translating the vision into an actionable mission that would be unique to the church's strengths.
- developing a set of strategies that would help the church overcome the major barriers in fulfilling the church's vision and its mission.

- setting forth the day-to-day and week-to-week activities that would help the church be effective in meeting the needs of its people.

A key learning for Jason was the fact that different people see the organization in different ways, with unique perspectives. These unique perspectives caused them to hear Jason's idea of the church's vision in different ways. He now understood that no matter how well he cast a vision, not all of the folks would hear and understand it. He felt challenged in a new way—a good way!

Finally, Jason was impressed that Bill had communicated these different perspectives in such a manner that the twenty-seven "retreaters" were able to get a good feel for their own perspectives. For example, the group figured that four of them were dreamers, five were "big project" types, seven were natural problem-solvers, and eleven were the kind of folks who just wanted to get the job done.

Jason now looked forward to the next step in the process— next month's meeting with the four dreamers, with the goal of developing a written vision statement for Creekside. Needless to say, Jason's entire outlook about Creekside had been transformed. He looked forward to a bright future at the helm of a healthy Creekside congregation!

PART III

Making the Planning Process Work in the Innovative Church

The *4D* paradigm for organizational planning sounds good! It starts with the organization's destination—its vision. It prescribes a healthy framework for mapping out the road to that destination, through the systematic development of missional, strategic, and tactical plans. The paradigm enables alignment between the organization's values and actions. It drives ownership among its members by encouraging their participation where they can be most effective.

The major question remains: "How does the organization actually get started?" This section deals with some of the "nuts and bolts" of putting the paradigm into practice.

7

Where Does Everyone Fit?

Not long ago my friend Rick and I were leading a workshop for a church leadership team. This particular church had gone through quite a bit in recent years. A thriving church fifteen to twenty years prior, their rate of growth had slowed significantly over the past few years. They had had numerous changes in senior pastoral leadership. A fire had significantly damaged the church facilities. They were meeting together with another church in town until repair on their facilities was completed.

As I moved through the presentation on the 4D paradigm of organizational planning, we discussed at length the attributes of the innovative congregation, drawing out the contrast to the bureaucratic congregation. It became quite apparent that the folks in the room were coming from quite different perspectives in the ways they thought about how church should be done.

For example, some of the folks felt their church had gotten stale by not doing anything new. Others felt that the church needed to stick closer to the traditional ways of doing things that had helped the church be so influential years ago. Some felt that the movement toward a more blended style of worship would lead to a "watering down" of the message of the Gospel. Some felt that worship style change was needed for the church to reach the changing demographic in its surrounding neighborhood. Needless to say, differing opinions abounded in the room!

Despite what seemed like a disjointedness among the folks in the room, I had a gut feeling that the church was still one with great resources and significant potential for rekindling much of the passion and energy that had previously driven it to great heights.

The Right People Will Lead to the Right Result

Before the session, I understood that this group in attendance was intended to be a visionary planning team. Knowing that churches have differing definitions of terms relating to planning, I was a bit skeptical of what the church was really trying to get out of the session.

We had gone through all of the four dimensions and were doing Q&A. By this time I had begun to guess how each of the team members' perspectives would slot into each of the four dimensions of planning. After getting a handle in my mind on who were dreamers and who were doers, I asked Steve, the leader of the group, "How was it determined that this group of people would be the ones here this weekend as the visionary planning team?" He replied, as if he knew where I was going, "These were the ones who sent their cards back in."

Our understanding was that the church was to go through a visionary planning process and that the folks in this room with us would constitute the group that would lead the church through the process. But this group was selected not by the way they saw things in terms of vision, mission, strategy, and tactics. Rather, it was more like a lottery approach. The church had sent out invitations to a multitude of its members. These fifteen or so had responded. They were great people, highly committed to their church and to Jesus Christ, but while I had pegged a couple of them as potentially visionary thinkers, they certainly weren't a visionary planning group.

Avoid the Temptation of Getting Everyone Involved

This situation illustrates an approach to planning that is common to many churches. We discussed the *open invitation approach* earlier. With the open invitation approach, churches try to involve as many people as possible in the planning process, often for the purposes of engaging many opinions and also for the purpose of driving ownership. The idea is that the more participants, the better the planning process.

Maximizing the number of participants is probably not the best course of action. As we said in chapter 1, "The danger of the *open invitation* is the possibility of having people involved in types of planning that they are not comfortable with, or equipped to, participate in. This can lead to ineffectiveness in the process and a faulty final product." Another rationale for the open invitation approach is the desire just to get enough people to participate to justify undergoing a planning process. The idea here is to maximize the pool of invitees so that out of that pool will come enough who will be able to participate. Apparently, Steve's church had taken this approach.

Getting the Right People Engaged

One of the largest challenges in any organization is the issue of getting the right people involved at the right level in the right job. For the purposes of developing visionary, missional, strategic, and tactical plans, the church must also take great care to staff each of the dimensions in an effective manner. In essence, the congregation's leaders must determine which folks will be most successful at each level and must engage them accordingly.

> ■ **One of the largest challenges in any organization is the issue of getting the right people involved at the right level, in the right job.**

A real key to leading others is the ability to drive ownership of the organization's values, direction, and projects into those who make up the organization. Top-level leaders can speak—even with great articulation—all they want about their ideas and their direction, but if those who hear their message don't adopt those ideas as their own and agree with the vision, values, and direction, then the organization's chances of success greatly diminish.

I have seen numerous situations in corporate and vocational ministry life that illustrate this principle: People in an organization are much more likely to take ownership in the organization's values, direction, and projects if they are allowed to participate in the process of developing those elements of the organization.

Developing a Pool of People

Determining which people in the organization should partici- pate in planning is often a difficult question. In many congregations, the "lead planners" are pretty much established by virtue of a place on a committee or board. Sometimes the people who give the most money are asked to serve. Often the idea is that we get their input on the table so the church can stand a better chance of keeping them—and their contributions—coming. Other churches take the position that membership rolls define the planners—i.e., all members are invited to participate, as with the *open invitation approach* we discussed before. Others have to scrounge around just to get enough people to move forward in a planning process.

A thorough planning process will take lots of effort and may require participants to restructure their own schedules while the process takes place. Those people who truly care about the church will stand out simply because their actions will demonstrate their commitment. They will be the most likely to give their time and resources to the process.

People of Passion and People of Position

George Bullard advocates a recognition of multiple groupings of people in the congregation based on the nature of their commitment:

> The People of Pastoral Leadership are the senior pastor, other ordained clergy, and primary program staff who form the pastoral leadership community of your congregation. They are the initiating leaders who comprise the core circle of leadership. They have the primary responsibility to cast God's vision for the congregation and to focus on its fulfillment... The People of Pastoral leadership represent approximately 1 percent of the active number of attending adults...
>
> The People of Passion are a minimum of 7 percent of the average number of active attending adults... This circle includes the People of Pastoral Leadership circle... The additional 6 percent have an obvious and contagious positive, spiritual passion about the future of the congregation... they are respected for their passion and willingness to act on their convictions out of a sincere devotion to God and to the congregation. They contribute greatly to the core spiritual journey of the congregation...
>
> The People of Position are a minimum of 21 percent of the average number of active attending adults... This circle includes the 1 percent People of Pastoral Leadership, plus the 6 percent People of Passion...
>
> People of Position hold one or more formal and informal leadership positions in the life of the congregation.

They are often visible leaders in the congregation and typically have been members of the congregation longer than the average member. They are generally stakeholders in the congregation and feel a deep sense of ownership, accountability, and responsibility for the past and present of the congregation. It is somewhat difficult for them to project the values of the past and present into the future. The People of Passion can be effective in influencing the openness of the People of Position to transition and change, but doing so is an art rather than a science...[1]

Bullard explains the potential influence of these groups among the rest of the congregation. He refers to the groups, collectively, as the Enduring Visionary Leadership Community.

If the Enduring Visionary Leadership Community becomes organized around God's emerging future for your congregation, your congregation will likely travel effectively in that direction. They clearly represent the necessary leadership of the congregation. It does not take a majority of your active congregation. It only requires the right 21 percent.[2]

Bullard's descriptions of the groups that comprise his Enduring Visionary Leadership Community can give us some guidelines in determining those who care the most about the church.

Other Considerations in Getting the Right People Engaged

In developing a pool of "the right people" for the planning process, it is always wise to look to the People of Pastoral Leadership, the People of Passion, and the People of Position. It is highly likely that in these groups those right people will be found. However, a couple of considerations could cause us to widen our search beyond those groups.

The Need for a Fresh Face

The people that come to mind when we think of the groups described by Bullard fall into those groups for a number of reasons, one of which probably has to do with their longevity in the congregation.

---

[1]George Bullard, *Pursuing the Full Kingdom Potential of Your Congregation* (St. Louis: Lake Hickory Resources, 2005), 44–46.
[2]Ibid., 47.

Certainly having the preponderance of the planning team composed of people with long tenure in the congregation is a positive thing. They are likely to have a wealth of knowledge and experience with the folks in the church and perhaps with the external environment of the church. As we have seen in the church I pastor, those who have been around for a long time easily forget how the person new to the church sees things.

■ **It is quite easy for those who have been around for a long time to forget how the person who is new to the church sees things.**

The "eyes" of the newcomers and their perception of the church are critical pieces of information that must factor significantly into the church's planning. A failure to recognize this could cause the church, over time, to lose touch with its external environment, causing it to become more inward-focused. For this reason, it may be good for the church's leaders to look at some of the newer folks in the congregation, those who have demonstrated the real potential for becoming people of passion in the future, but who perhaps have not yet had the opportunity to serve in any significant leadership positions. However, some risks are associated with engaging some of the less-proven folks in a congregation:

- They may carry a hidden, self-serving agenda that has not yet had time to come to the surface.
- Their spiritual maturity may not be to the level needed to participate in such an important endeavor.
- Inadequate interpersonal skills may cause them to have difficulty serving as a part of a team.
- Their inability for productive interaction could drag the performance of the rest of the team down.

However, people with fresh perspectives *can* be valuable in the planning process.

Allowance for a Participant's Time Constraints

I believe in the adage that goes something like this: "*Busy people are busy because they get things done. Because they get things done, they get called on a lot to do things.*" I will add this slight qualification: This description fits busy people who are *also productive*. In the long run, only productive people—those who usually *get it right*—will be asked to do things. If we are going to pull these busy, but productive, people into the planning process, they will have to be asked. They will also have other things going on, both within and outside the church, as they multitask, spin multiple plates, etc. This "busy person issue" poses a real challenge for the congregation. Often the "busy people" are among our very best people—the ones we want to be involved in major decisions and planning in the church.

■ Often the "busy people" are among our very best people—the ones we want to be involved in major decisions and planning in the church.

To leave them out would cost the church access to some real wisdom, expertise, and energy. To include them may mean the team cannot move as quickly due to their limited accessibility. The decision must be made up front, then, whether to invite "busy people" into the process. In the vast majority of situations, the answer will be to include them, while making allowances that will minimize inconveniences on the rest of the participants.

So, the church will likely need to make adjustments to enable the participation of its very best people!

Everybody Has a Place

Developing a pool of potentially right candidates to include in the planning process is only a beginning step. Next, the leadership has to determine how each of the people should best be utilized. Here careful consideration must be made with regard to the individuality of each person. Perhaps the key element of successful planning within each of the four dimensions is the accurate assignment of participants into each of the four dimensions.

For the most part, many in the organization will fit fairly nicely into one of the four dimensions of planning in terms of their perspective—the way they see things. For example, those we may classify as "big picture people" will likely fit best in the visionary planning dimension, and perhaps the missional planning dimension. These are people who generally have big ideas or have vivid imaginations.

Everyone will likely fit. The operative question is, "Where—in which dimension—will each of them fit?"

Finding the Fit

✔ Those who are visionaries are really no more important than the strategists or the doers. All the participants are important.

When I present the "Four Dimensions of Planning" process, I like to show it in the form of a pyramid. The pyramid is divided

The 4D Paradigm
Key Questions and Planning Horizons

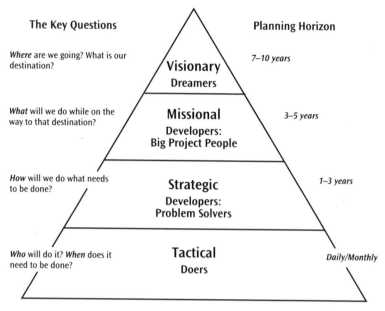

The Key Questions

Where are we going? What is our destination?

What will we do while on the way to that destination?

How will we do what needs to be done?

Who will do it? *When* does it need to be done?

Visionary
Dreamers

Missional
Developers:
Big Project People

Strategic
Developers:
Problem Solvers

Tactical
Doers

Planning Horizon

7–10 years

3–5 years

1–3 years

Daily/Monthly

The Four Dimensions of Planning

into four sections, with the height of each section roughly the same. The pyramid starts with vision at the top, followed by missional planning, strategic planning, and then tactical planning at the bottom. The purpose of the pyramid is not to demonstrate any type of hierarchical relationship. Visionaries are really no more important than the strategists or the doers. All the participants are important.

Rather, the purpose of the pyramid is to illustrate two things:

1. The natural sequencing of the dimensions. For example, mission flows out of vision. Strategies can't be developed until the mission(s) of the organization are clearly defined. Tactical planning done on a day-to-day basis can't be developed until the strategies have been set forth. So, *the four dimensions are sequential.*
2. An estimate of the *relative proportion of people whose perspectives coincide with each of the four dimensions.* For

example, tactical planning is reflected as the base of the pyramid. More people fit here, as *doers or tacticians,* than in any of the other dimensions. Likewise, fewer people are missional-thinking than strategists, and still fewer are true visionaries.

◼ **There are fewer missional-thinking people than strategists, and there are fewer true visionaries than any of the other categories.**

Staffing the Four Dimensions

From among the pool of potential planning participants, the leadership must do its best to determine into which of the four dimensions each of their people fit. This process may be somewhat time-consuming. Any organization had best think about where its people would each fit in terms of the dimensions. That information should be kept in a database. As we discussed earlier, planning should not be a discrete exercise, or a one-time or even periodic activity. Through each visionary and missional cycle, through each strategic initiative and each daily work plan, organizational members must keep in mind the continuous nature of the planning process.

A Word of Caution

Congregations must take extra care in discerning the motives of potential participants in the planning process—particularly when it comes to folks who are relatively new to the church. Often churches are havens for frustrated churchgoers who want to have influence, but who don't have the platform for influence at work or in some other organizational context. These people often have inflated self-concepts, and their motives are more about themselves and less about helping the congregation move forward. These people may move from congregation to congregation until they can find a context in which they will be allowed to hold a position, or to have a place of influence with the pastor, elders, or other key leaders.

◼ **Often churches are havens for frustrated churchgoers who want to have influence, but who don't have the platform for influence at work or in some other organizational context.**

Our church certainly fell into a rut, particularly in our early days, when we allowed these folks to take root in our church. In starting a new church, particularly one that experiences rapid growth, a common temptation is to welcome anyone who appears to have experience to serve in a ministry role. We often succumb to the idea that "any warm, breathing body will do—particularly if they tithe." This is a dangerous position to take, especially given the fact that newer churches are often landing places for prior churchgoers who were disgruntled, for whatever reason, at their previous churches. It takes lots of time and energy—time and energy a busy new church planter/pastor rarely has—to check out thoroughly the church people who begin attending. Of course, this happens not only in new church starts. A similar situation may just as easily arise in churches that successfully transition from traditional to more contemporary approaches. It doesn't take much to attract a crowd. But it sure takes a lot to keep one.

Over the years, our church has paid the price of moving too quickly to put any and all willing churchgoers into places of service—without doing our homework on them. The results usually didn't show up quickly. But invariably, in a great many of these situations, it eventually became clear that some of these members were more interested in furthering their own ideas than the mission of the church. On occasion, this trend revealed folks who tried to *hijack the vision* of our church.

Our often naïve staffing approach proved especially costly when we experienced the first of two major crashes in the church's first six years. Some disgruntled (as it turned out) churchgoers who were new to our church were placed into roles of service, and, ultimately, leadership. Some of them banded together in an undercover operation to hijack the vision of our church and to remove me from the lead pastor role. The result was not pretty, as our church went through a miserable year, losing 30 percent of the congregation and a proportionate level of income. The bright side was that a strong group of elders handled the situation reasonably well. We learned many lessons, but great damage was done—mostly because of moving people too quickly to staff positions of leadership.

The bottom line is that church leadership should get to know their folks as much as possible. This helps tremendously in making good decisions in staffing the planning process.

Their Fit: The Visionaries

A true sense of vision is critical to the life of any individual, and any organization. Proverbs 29:18 affirms this" "Where there is no vision, the people perish: but he that keepeth the law, happy is he" (KJV).

■ Leaders can be leaders with or without this visionary gift. But having the visionary gift certainly doesn't ensure that one is a leader.

The language in this verse doesn't necessarily emphasize a physical death ("the people perish") as much as it does a sense of discouragement. The idea is that having a clear vision—a foresight, mental ability to see a clear destination—is motivational, again to an individual and to any group of people. Real visionaries are perhaps the rarest of thinkers. Real visionaries are a subset of the group we have already described as *dreamers*. Dreamers often have a difficult time communicating with others because their imaginations are so active. People may become frustrated because they sense that the dreamers are not practical. Dreamers can be tough to deal with because they think at 30,000 feet cruising altitude, a level that most others simply can't reach.

A common idea is that the visionaries are found at the top of the organization chart in the highest levels of leadership. The reality is leaders can be leaders with or without this *visionary gift*. Having the visionary gift certainly doesn't ensure that one is a leader. *Leaders are leaders primarily because others follow them. For others to follow, the leader must know his or her direction and have the ability to communicate enough of the particulars of that direction to others, so they can know how to follow.*

Identifying the Real Visionaries

Finding the visionaries in the organization is usually not a difficult task. We need first to look for *those folks who think big*! Visionaries may typically have a difficult time focusing on the here and now. In their day-to-day tasks, they may not always be very efficient. They may think about the roles of others more than they should, simply because they have broader perspectives.

The real visionaries, those whom the organization will want engaged in the planning process, will be able to relate to the current reality of the organization and its environment. They will then likely be able to integrate that understanding of the current reality with their imagination to formulate an attainable vision—one that the organization can actually achieve. The vision, then, becomes credible.

■ Visionaries will likely be able to integrate the understanding of the current reality with their imagination in order to formulate an attainable vision.

Real visionaries will have at least some ability to present the dreams so that others can understand. Real visionaries will also likely have a track record of performance in the organization. They will have earned credibility among colleagues and superiors, simply because of their prior success.

Let's clarify a very important point: *Not all dreamers are visionaries*. An organization can be highly frustrated by dreamers who don't have a clear picture of the organization and "dream out of context." These dreamers may just like the attention that comes with having big ideas, whether they are relevant or not. Sometimes their ideas seem to be so "knee jerk" and so far out that they don't seem to be tied into any reality. They may truly have a sincere desire to influence the organization positively, but may not yet have the experience, the understanding, or the credibility to have a good handle on the current reality of the organization. The leaders in the organization must be careful to distinguish between the dreamers and real visionaries.

Lessons Learned about Dreamers

I learned this lesson the hard way a few years ago. One of our church's staff—a dynamite guy with talent and maturity—left to pursue another line of ministry. We ultimately staffed his position with someone who was new to the church staff role, but nevertheless a very solid person with great potential, and the ability to really think big! One of the many great things about our new staff member is passion for building deep relationships of accountability within the body of Christ. The staff person brought a wonderful new perspective to our team.

Soon after the new staff person came on, we scheduled a staff retreat—mainly to get to know each other within the context of the new team composition and to discuss how we would work together. An even more specific objective for the retreat was to assimilate the new team member with the rest of the team. For the retreat I chose to use *The Five Dysfunctions of a Team* assessment process, based on Patrick Lencioni's book by the same name.[3] This resource, by the way, is a fantastic team-building tool for nearly any team situation.

One of the five dysfunctions in Lencioni's model is the *absence of trust* among team members. On our self-assessments at the retreat, I was shocked when our team's composite scores reflected

---

[3]Patrick Lencioni, *The Five Dysfunctions of a Team* (San Francisco: Jossey-Bass, 2002).

a much lower than expected result for our team's level of trust—an area in which I had thought we were very strong. As it turned out, the composite score was dragged down by the assessment of the new staff member, whose idea of trust was built around that passion for deep, enduring, and even intimate relationships among believers.

I really should have seen this coming, but I didn't. When we discussed the results, the staff member opened up concerning the fact that we had only just come together as a team, and so we couldn't have the trust level that would drive us toward high performance. We simply would have to spend much more time together before we could reach that level. While the logic of the argument made lots of sense, I failed to bring the point, and discussion, into context. As a result, the conversation on trust/ distrust lingered. Other staff members brought out issues of trust/ distrust in our earlier experiences together—issues that had been previously worked and resolved, so I thought—and continued to elaborate on them. The result was a preoccupation with past events that had (again, I thought) long been taken care of. Needless to say, the whole retreat lost traction, and little was accomplished.

What was the real problem? Was it the staff member bringing up and elaborating on the elusive nature of real trust among a group of people just coming together? No! The real problem was my inability to consider that person's perspective on relationship (and I was certainly aware of it). I should have known that the trust/ distrust element of Lencioni's *Five Dysfunctions* tool would need to be addressed. I should perhaps have taken steps to lower the group's expectations around the issue of trust, given the brevity of the staff member's tenure, and the passion for deep relationship.

My biggest lesson from that retreat, though, had to do with the difference between dreamers and real visionaries. I learned that our new partner, while a very valuable staff team member, was, in fact, a dreamer, not a real visionary. The overriding passion for depth in relationships and the commitment to the time required for that to happen led to big dreams about intense community within the church, and particularly the new staff member's specific area of ministry. But that passion led to an inability to see the bigger picture of the team and of the organization—the church—as a whole. This inability to see that big picture kept that staff person from having legitimate vision for the church as a whole.

Fortunately, soon after that retreat experience we came to this realization, and were able to leverage this individual's passions, so that this person could have a productive tenure with us. However, I always had to remember that I was dealing with a dreamer who was not a visionary.

Organizational leadership must be very careful to distinguish the real visionaries in the organization. Again, not all dreamers are real visionaries. Real visionaries understand context. They will have credibility built by a track record of performance and some tenure in the organization. The dreams of real visionaries can lead the organization toward a very positive, and even attainable, future.

Missional Thinkers

The dreams of visionaries can, and often do, frustrate others in the organization. Translators, then, are needed. These translators can "interpret" the dreams of the visionary and help bring those dreams to a level—maybe 20,000 feet altitude—at which these dreams can be effectively communicated to others in the organization. This is the point, when there is accurate and articulate communication of the dreams, that vision comes into view.

This first level of translation comes with the missional thinkers that we discussed in chapter 4. These are the folks in the organization who can grasp the issues surrounding the key question of, "What will we do while we are on our way toward our destination (the vision)?" Keep in mind the three major criteria for an effective mission: *(1) an action orientation, (2) a well-defined completion point, and (3) the incorporation of the uniqueness of the organization.* These missional thinkers must be able to determine and define the major courses for action that will be required for the vision to come to reality.

Finding the Missional Thinkers

The missional thinkers in an organization can usually be found by addressing the following questions:

- "Who are the big project people in an organization?"
- "Who are the people who have taken on big projects or tasks and have been successful?"
- "Who are the folks to whom others go when they have a big task to accomplish?"

When these questions are considered, the identity of the missional thinkers will usually become fairly obvious. They will be the directors of the very successful capital campaign in the church.

In the manufacturing company, they will be the ones who led the team in moving a strategic product to market ahead of schedule. In the consulting firm, they may be the ones who took on the task of expanding the firm's business into an entirely new market sector.

Missional thinkers are often motivated by the "bigness" of a project. They love the challenge of leading the charge in moving the organization forward by quantum leaps, and are typically not satisfied with incremental forward movement. They often love to multitask and are usually the very busy people in the organization. This busy-ness often comes as a result of being recruited to work in areas because of their significant abilities to see things through to accomplishment.

■ **Missional thinkers are often motivated by the "bigness" of a project.**

While missional thinkers may be more numerous in an organization than real visionaries, the general population still has relatively few missional thinkers. Thus you expect to have few in the organization. Based on my observations in working in the corporate world and with churches and church leaders, I would estimate that no more than 5–15 percent of the population are real visionaries, and no more than 20 percent of the population are true missional thinkers. This relationship is reflected in the pyramid illustration of the 4D paradigm, with the missional thinkers depicted in the second (from the top) segment of the pyramid.

Protecting the Missional Thinkers

Often, the missional thinkers have a tough time saying "no" to things simply because they get a "rush" by getting things done. The more projects in which they can be involved, the greater their sense of accomplishment and the greater their level of significance. Because these missional thinkers have a tough time saying "no," they can often get overextended.

■ **Organizations, then, must be quite protective of their missional thinkers. Their time and energy are critical to the organization's success.**

One common result in smaller organizations, particularly churches, is that when organizational leadership perceives a high priority need and wants to tap one of these key missional thinkers to lead a major project or initiative, they may have to be pulled off other, less-important projects. These less-important projects, however, may still have great value to the organization. Reassigning the missional thinker to lead the higher impact project, while necessary, could cause a loss of momentum for the smaller projects. Organizations, then, must be quite protective of their missional thinkers. Their time and energy are critical to the organization's success.

The Strategic Thinkers

Once the missional thrusts of the organization have been established, the missional thinkers must make a clean handoff to the strategists. The strategists then break down the broad plan for action that the mission sets forth into a more clear, and detailed, specific course of action. These plans of action, the strategies, will tend to focus more at the departmental levels, closer to the daily operations of the organization.

While the missional thinkers focus on the big projects that support the fulfillment of the organization's vision, the strategists answer the "how to" questions in the organization. They deal with the finer details of the mission and work to define plans for accomplishing the organization's missional initiatives.

Finding the Strategists

Strategic thinkers are really at a premium. While perhaps not as rare as visionaries and missional thinkers, good strategists may be difficult to find. To find the best strategic thinkers in the organization, *leadership should look for its best problem-solvers.* Leadership can look to the natural tendencies of its people, as well as track records of performance, to ascertain those who have potential for being good strategists.

Problem-solvers typically have good analytical abilities. They are often able to look at organizational situations and determine whether or not the organization is producing at maximum capacity. If the organization is not producing at that maximum, the problem-solver can often look deeper into the situation to figure out the source of the inefficiencies.

Typically, when things aren't going just right in an organization, focus seems to turn to the outward signs of problems. These signs usually reflect symptoms rather than the actual problems. Good problem-solvers are able to discern the difference between symptoms and the actual problems. They have a natural ability to "peel back the layers of the onion" to get to the core issues, where the problem can be detected, defined, and addressed.

■ **Good problem-solvers are able to discern the difference between symptoms and the actual problems.**

Keeping Problem-solvers Focused

Because a problem-solving approach is often by nature somewhat detail-oriented, problem-solvers can become too focused on problems that may not be significant to the organization's success. Because problem-solvers are likely to have a narrower focus, they will need help in staying focused on issues that are in fact significant to the fulfillment of the organization's vision—those things that are "mission-critical."

The handoff between the missional thinkers and the strategists comes into play here. The strategists' agenda should be driven by the missional thrusts developed by the missional thinkers. The missional thinkers should, then, be careful to pass to the strategists a clearly defined set of missional plans. Leadership should hold strategists accountable for working within the boundaries of these missional plans.

Good strategists also tend to be good communicators to both the missional thinkers as well as to the doers who make things happen in the organization. Again, the strategists are the second level of developers in the organization. As missional thinkers translate primarily between visionaries and strategists, strategists translate between missional thinkers and the doers at the tactical level.

The Tacticians: Finishing the Job!

As stated previously, at the tactical level things are less about planning and more about simply getting things done! No matter the quality of visionary, missional, and strategic plans, they cannot be successful without effective execution. The best-laid plans are often rendered useless by inattention to detail, apathy, ignorance, and incompetence. Therefore, the handoff between strategists and those responsible for execution is critical. This handoff probably has less margin for error than in the handoffs between visionaries and missional thinkers and between missional thinkers and strategists. At this level, which is often the one closest to the customer/client, precision is very important.

Finding the Tacticians

The best tacticians, or doers, will have technical competence. Without the knowledge of their function or role and how to carry it out, they will be of limited value to the organization. In the previous chapter we looked at some of the major character trends desirable in a tactician—*focus, responsibility, interpersonal skills, a specialty, initiative.* Of course, you need to look for other attributes in tacticians. Most of these are certainly desirable for any and every member of the organization. Because of the tacticians' close proximity to those who receive the goods and services of the organization, it is especially critical that they have these qualities. Just a few of these attributes are...

- *Attention to Detail.* The best tacticians understand the precision with which their jobs must be carried out, and the small margin for error. In contrast, visionaries and missional thinkers work within much broader levels of organizational perspective.
- *Dependability.* Because the tactical level is the closest to the customer/client and because there is little margin for error, the organization must seek out people who are highly dependable. This dependability encompasses the principles of work ethic, promptness and timeliness, and a willingness to do what it takes to get the job done.
- *Integrity.* Integrity is all about consistency, authenticity, and the willingness to follow through on commitments. It is especially important that an organization place direct responsibility for getting a product or service to its customers/clients in the hands of those who can be counted on to do what they say they will do.
- *Discernment.* Tacticians also need to have a sense of judgment. They need to be able to handle situations in which they must interface with customers, clients, etc., simply because they will likely be the ones in the organization with the most intimate knowledge of the customer/client relationship and the use of the product or service provided by the organization.
- *Diplomacy.* The responsibility of interfacing with the customer/client often falls on the shoulders of tacticians. They will have to deal with both pleasant and unpleasant situations relating to those customers/clients. Therefore they will need to be able to communicate effectively, with calmness and consistency.

Pulling It Together

Effective staffing of each dimension of planning is critical. It is important that each participant work in the dimension of planning most natural to him or her. For example, it will be dangerous to have someone who likes to work in the details trying to put together the vision and mission (and maybe the strategy) of the organization. Likewise, having a leader who sees things at a visionary level working at the day-to-day tactical level can be similarly frustrating.

Figuring out who fits where in an organization is not an easy task. A few guidelines can be helpful in the process. For example, the real visionaries are dreamers who have an understanding of the organization, its context, and the interrelationships within the organization. Missional thinkers are best found by looking for people who have taken on leading big projects and have been successful. The best strategists have strong problem-solving skills, highlighted by an ability to cut through symptoms and to get straight to the problem issues. They typically understand the organization's context and have an ability to know how the organization as a whole works. Tacticians must be technically competent and able to work with a large degree of independence. Usually, they are the closest to the customer/client/parishioner in an organization, and they have to be trusted to make quality decisions so that these relationships are maximized.

8

Where Does the Leader Fit?

My friend Rick and I finally broke through with the church's planning team we described in the previous chapter. The team seemed haphazardly put together. During the early part of the session we helped the group understand their different perspectives and how each could fit neatly into the four dimensions of planning. It was a really neat group of folks, just not a visionary planning team. I was especially impressed with the leader of the group, Steve, who, I assumed, was the senior pastor of the church.

An "aha! moment" in the session appeared during the second half. Steve seemed to carry himself with great security, yet with great humility. He seemed to receive great respect from the rest of the group, but still fit in as a group member—not so much as *the* leader. When Steve would speak, which didn't occur often, the rest of the group would stop whatever they were doing and listen attentively. Whatever Steve said would shift the focus of the discussion, as the other folks would follow his lead. His influence among the group was quite evident. I assumed that Steve's influence on the group was healthy, but I wanted to get to know him a bit better. So I spoke to him at length during a break. I heard him state his passion for the church and its ability to influence its environment. I heard him speak of his love for the people in the room and those back home. After talking with Steve, I could understand why his people respected him so much. I came to feel really good about Steve the Leader!

Soon the discussion turned to the issue of leadership in the church. It became pretty evident that a number of the folks in the room were not too happy with the senior pastoral leadership situation. I became increasingly uncomfortable as I began to wonder what Steve might be thinking of this conversation. I thought that the group had been, up to this point, so respecting of him. As a matter of fact, I thought that some of their comments had seemed to tout Steve as being able to walk on water! How could I have misread this situation so badly? As I looked at him out of the corner of my eye, though, I could see that he was unfazed.

The conversation continued around the theme of the senor pastoral position not providing the leadership the church required. Then, Steve joined in on the conversation and provided some clarifying comments. But he had me asking in my mind, *"If you knew about these issues, why haven't you made any changes?"* I then asked Steve a clarifying question—one posed in such a way that it was obvious that I thought Steve was the senior pastor.

At my question, Steve laughed and said, "No, I'm not the senior pastor. I'm the associate pastor." After I regained my composure, someone in the group went on to explain to me that the church had had something like four different senior pastors in the past twenty or so years. He went on to chronicle the experiences they had had with each one, along with the great disappointment the church experienced when they had left. I realized that while I had heard a lot of comments thus far in the meeting, my impression was that the church had held its ground pretty well. They suffered some setbacks along the way, along with perhaps some reluctance to move forward when some opportunities had arisen. This didn't sound like a church that had been through such significant senior leadership changes.

Then something hit me. I looked at Steve and I asked, "How long have you been at the church in your associate pastor role?" He responded that he had been there a little over twenty years, and that he was quite content with his role and this position. So I immediately made the statement to the group: "These senior pastors who have come and gone in your church have not been the leaders for your church. Steve is the real leader of your church, and he has been for some time."

I was surprised to hear what I heard next—nothing! The group sat there, obviously processing my statement. Then slowly, they began to look at each other, nodding their heads in agreement, realizing that indeed Steve was the real leader in the church. Even Steve himself was taken aback by the discussion. While I don't think Steve had a problem with seeing himself as *a* leader, my guess is that he never really had seen himself as *the* leader in his church.

A Leadership Shortage? Too Many Churches?

Pastors take on lead positions in today's congregations, almost always with great expectations of both themselves and the congregations they serve. All too often things don't work out. Often the problems lie with the congregations they serve. At times pastors find they just do not seem to have what it takes to lead. Guiding a congregation in a lead or solo pastor role is quite a challenge. A pastor has to be many things to many people. Even more important, he or she has to lead the congregation from an organizational perspective. Whether you consider leadership to be a spiritual gift, an innate ability, or a learned skill, it is absolutely necessary for heading up any type of organization. To have a leadership-deficient pastor in a role requiring strong organizational leadership will harm a congregation. Unfortunately, real leadership seems to be rare among lead pastors today. As a result, two relevant questions need to be addressed:

1. Are there too many individual, disconnected congregations in America?
2. Are pastors, in general, really that ill-equipped to lead the congregations of today?

■ **To have a leadership-deficient pastor in a role requiring strong organizational leadership will be harmful to a congregation.**

The proliferation of congregations in America has led to a crisis. (Of course, we need new congregations to reach people for the kingdom of God!) So many congregations have lead pastors who are simply not gifted with the ability to provide organizational leadership. Pastors who have no clue about the gift of leadership are forced into leading, simply because the position calls for it. This causes great stress, stunted growth, and often failure for both the pastor and the congregation.

This situation creates a vicious cycle.

First, while leadership-deficient pastors placed in such positions need, and may even want, to develop leadership skills, they simply don't know how. Not gifted in that manner, they just don't have the capacity to develop leadership skills.

Second, often the congregation assumes that a pastor is naturally a leader. As a result, the congregation doesn't support the pastor's efforts to seek leadership development opportunities. Helpful conferences and coaching sessions may be viewed simply as time away from the job.

Third, a leadership-deficient lead pastor is unlikely to have anyone within the congregation to help him or her become more leadership-proficient. He or she could benefit from having a supervising pastor who is strong on leadership, one who can serve as a mentor and coach.

■ **Often a general assumption in the congregation is that a pastor is naturally a leader.**

Fourth, the pastor may not be able to develop what leadership gifts are present because so much energy is sucked out in trying to lead. Being forced to do things outside our natural strengths drains us of emotional and physical energy. The result is usually a frustrated pastor, who might otherwise function very well in a different context.

As director of a leadership development organization for congregational leaders, I see many of my friends affected this way. They are good people, most often very gifted—but maybe not equipped for the organizational leadership side of the role. The deficit of pastors who are leaders is quite significant in American churches. Compounding the situation, many pastors have seriously considered leaving vocational ministry, primarily due to conflict with congregation members. Therefore, the paucity of pastors gifted in leadership will remain significant unless some dramatic changes are made.

The Desire of an Organization to Have a Leader

Now, back to my day with Steve and his church's "ad hoc visionary planning team." Why would I make the assumption that Steve was the senior pastor? Why would I later make the claim that Steve was, as the "No. 2" guy in the church, the real leader of the church? Another way of asking the question is this: *What makes a group of people willing to follow a leader?* Thinking of Steve and his group, I observed at least five things that day.

1. Steve's group seemed truly to want a leader at the helm.
2. The group members were very responsive to Steve as the leader.
3. These folks would respond to informal leadership more than they would respond to positional leadership.
4. They placed realistic expectations on Steve.
5. They really seemed to value Steve's leadership continuity.

The first reason I had assumed Steve was the senior pastor really had more to do with the planning group than it had to do with Steve. I saw, quite obviously, *that the rest of the group actually viewed him as the leader.* They stopped their sidebar conversations and listened to him when he spoke. They answered his questions with seriousness, not with the joking around that typically goes on in informal settings. They obviously *followed him,* and it was quite a natural thing for them to do. But Steve may have never seen it that way—until that day.

Perhaps even more significant than Steve's actual leadership was *his planning group's—and I assume his congregation's—deep desire for their pastor to be the leader!* They saw Steve as their leader because he, in effect, had been their true pastor!

■   **"Does the church see the pastor as the leader or as the hired hand?"**

One of the key questions I always lay out for pastors when we discuss the 4D paradigm is this: "Does the church see the pastor as the leader or as the hired hand?" The way the pastor answers the question says a lot about whether the pastor will have the authority to even begin to lead the church to make any changes, much less doing something so significant as incorporating *4D.*

The Hired Hand

When I think of a hired hand, I think of Eb in the old comedy *Green Acres.* He was the goofy farmhand who gave Mr. Douglas such a hard time with his off-beat—but often hilarious—ideas and responses to Mr. Douglas' questions. While the nonsensical nature of this TV character was quite exaggerated, it depicted quite a gap between Mr. Douglas, the refined big city attorney turned farm owner, and Eb, the likely uneducated, largely uninformed employee.

In so many churches, the congregation drives the decision-making process. A system known as the *congregational form of government* is based on the very idea that the members of the church have the say in the church's larger decisions—typically through a voting process. This form of government obviously places a high premium on church membership, which is usually the means to *have a vote.*

The congregational form of government is largely built on the idea of a democratic governmental system. In such a system, at least in theory, everyone who holds citizenship gets to vote on matters of government. The system in our nation, which is largely a representative democracy, works pretty well—for our nation. Built-in checks and balances such as, among other things, the distinct three branches of government add to the effectiveness of our system.

■ **Any person in an organizational leadership capacity must have the credibility to lead. And there must be opportunity for the leaders to earn that credibility.**

Such a system is not necessarily the best form of government for a local church. The pastor is usually the person most familiar with the issues facing the church, but too often in churches with a congregational form of government, the church has basically pushed the pastor out of any major decision-making. The irony, then, is that when voting is used to make the decisions, most of those who in effect make the decisions through their votes may be the ones least knowledgeable of the issues actually confronting the church.

Pastor Eb

In churches overly focused on the congregational form of government, the pastor can easily be relegated to a role of "hired hand." This "hired hand" status can be extreme. I recently heard a pastor describe this admonishment from the deacon board, just after he arrived to assume the pastorate at his church: "We just want you to know that you're not in charge here. The church makes the decisions, and we hired you to follow those decisions and to carry them out." Ouch!

Any person in an organizational leadership capacity must have the credibility to lead. At the same time, the organization must provide *opportunity* for the leaders to earn that credibility. A church overly focused on a congregational form of government may never give a pastor the opportunity to earn that credibility. The pastor often winds up as the *hired hand*. Of course, many pastors simply are not leaders, as we have already said. Those who are not naturally gifted as leaders and who are honest in their self-assessment may feel fine about being, and function perfectly well as, the hired hand.

The great commitment that is required for a church to move through *4D* necessitates *strong pastoral leadership*. Before strong pastoral leadership can be exercised, the church must create a climate conducive to the exercise of that strong pastoral leadership. The church must be ready to follow that leadership. Unfortunately, in a church that sees its pastor as a hired hand, such a climate is highly unlikely to exist.

The Leader Pastor

Some churches, by nature, see their pastor as their hired hand. Others, like Steve's church, truly see their pastor, or want to see their pastor, as their leader. A church that naturally sees its pastor as a leader will more likely have a "big picture" perspective of its identity. Such a church will allow the pastor greater opportunity to earn the credibility required to take the church through significant transition, crisis, etc. Such a church will give the pastor more flexibility in presenting and implementing his or her own ideas. That church will be more likely to follow a pastor with leadership abilities.

Conversely, a pastor will have a very difficult time in moving the church forward in the *4D* process when that pastor is not seen as a leader. A church that desires to begin afresh the process of visioning and developing its mission, strategies, and tactical plans will require strong leadership at the helm.

Responsiveness to the Leader

Steve's planning group *actually listened to him*. To a person, they stopped what they were doing and seemed to genuinely care about what he said. Before a church—or any organization, for that matter—can truly move forward, it must have real leadership, and the organization's members must allow the leaders to lead. Will they be right on every decision? No. But the organization must expect leadership. Members must help leaders fulfill their leadership responsibilities. The organization, then, must be willing to respond to the leader. At the same time, the leader must inspire the organization to be willing to respond. It's a two-way street.

■ **The organization must be willing to respond to the leader. At the same time, the leader must inspire the organization to be willing to respond.**

Following the Leader

I've heard the definition time and again: "A leader is only a leader if he or she has someone following." We often forget that fact. To be "follow-able," at a minimum the leader must focus on two aspects of the organization's direction: forward movement and alignment.

Forward Movement

A true leader is *knowledgeable* enough about the organization to understand its direction and *influential* enough to help the organizational members move in that direction. The technical giftedness among organizational leaders may differ, but they are able to transcend their own abilities and limitations to move the organization forward through their influence with others in the organization.

Alignment Among the Four Dimensions

Any organization needs to have constant check-ups with regard to the degree of alignment among the four dimensions of planning. Alignment involves a clarity of organizational direction and action with regard to the organization's movement. For example, someone shooting a rifle at a target, looking through its scope, must be sure of alignment between his or her line of sight, the crosshairs in the scope, and the target. Likewise, the leader must keep the organization focused on the target, and must ensure that organizational members view the target similarly—through the same scope!

Earlier we discussed handoffs between visionaries and missional thinkers, between missional thinkers and strategists, and between strategists and tacticians, or doers. A goal of alignment is to ensure directional and actionable consistency among the perceptions of all the members. If strategists misconstrue or misinterpret missional plans they receive from missional thinkers, strategic plans can be developed under different assumptions than those used in developing the missional plans. This misalignment can take the organization away from its intended course of action.

■ Alignment occurs when there is a clarity of organizational direction and action with regard to the organization's movement.

A good way to test the alignment of the organization is to survey a random sampling of organizational members, representative of the organization's mix of visionaries, missional thinkers, strategists, and tacticians. Leaders should then ask some simple questions around awareness of the organization's direction at visionary, missional, and strategic levels. The answers will give a good indication as to whether the organization is aligned.

Informal vs. Positional Leadership

The situation with Steve and his group illustrated a third very strong point: *people respond better to informal leadership than they respond to positional leadership.* Positional leadership is based on the authority to direct others who are lower on the organizational totem pole. This authority comes as a result of placement within an organizational structure; positional leadership does not necessarily require real leadership. The term "positional leadership" in many cases is an oxymoron. This is because many managers lead based on the level of their particular job. They leverage their position to direct others to perform in the organizational context.

Organizations in which positional leadership is emphasized are often characterized by some or all of the following:

Micromanagement

Managers in higher-level organization positions frequently gain security and status by making an inordinate amount of the decisions, and imposing those decisions on those at lower organizational levels. Committees, for example, are notorious for making decisions and policies to be carried out at lower levels of the organization. Micromanagement occurs whenever decisions are made at organizational levels higher than necessary. For example, an organization characterized by micromanagement may require top-level executives to scrutinize and often approve many entry level hiring decisions. The executives may have no direct knowledge of the positions and their requirements. Often this level of approval adds only bureaucratic red tape and time to a process—time that is valuable to the organization's ability to be responsive to its clients/customers.

Low Levels of Incentive/Initiative

In many organizations, positional leadership is based on rules and regulations, often known as policies and procedures. These "R&R"/"P&P"s may be written or unwritten. The perception of success in the organization is based on adherence to those rules and regulations. Often, little room is left for the discretion of members themselves in making decisions. As a result, organizations like these provide little incentive for creativity.

Followership by Fear

Positional leadership often leads to followership by fear, characterized by members having to "get on board" with even bad ideas just because the person giving orders is above them in the organization. The way of dealing with subordinates in this context is often heavy-handed, with more emphasis on retribution for falling short of performance objectives than on rewards for meeting and exceeding objectives.

Organizations in which these three elements are common will be largely unhealthy. A business, church, athletic team, etc., will not be successful in the long run with a culture of positional leadership. Such an organization thwarts its people and their creativity, leading to low morale and high turnover.

A Better Way

Real leaders know a better way! Informal leadership is about *real influence, which is the core of effective leadership.* Real influence is based on the leader and how the leader treats followers. The bottom line is this: Real leaders don't need a position from which to exert their leadership abilities. They will be leaders regardless of their position—even if they don't have a position in the organization.

■ **Real leaders don't need a position from which to exert their leadership abilities.**

John Maxwell speaks at length about "The Position Myth" of leadership:[1]

> If I had to identify the number one misconception people have about leadership, it would be that leadership comes simply from having a position or a title. But nothing could be further from the truth. You don't need to possess a position at the top of your group, department, division, or organization to lead.

Maxwell goes on to refer to his *Five Levels of Leadership* model. About the first level, called *Position,* he states:

> People follow because they have to… Your influence will not extend beyond the lines of your job description. The longer you stay here, the higher the turnover and the lower the morale.

The second leadership level he refers to as *Permission.* At this level, it's about relationships. Of this level, he writes:

> People follow because they want to. People will follow you beyond your stated authority. This level allows work to be fun… Staying too long on this level without rising will cause highly motivated people to become restless.

---

[1] John Maxwell, *The 360° Leader* (Nashville: Thomas Nelson, 2005), 5.

At the third level, called *Production,* results are very important. Maxwell states:

> People follow because of what you have done for the organization… This is where success is sensed by most people. They like you and what you are doing. Problems are fixed with very little effort because of momentum.

Maxwell identifies two further leadership levels—*People Development* and *Personhood.* These two levels, respectively, are characterized by development of other leaders and the respect that a leader gains over years of growing people and organizations.

Real Influence

Real influence, then, is all about how one carries himself or herself in terms of affecting others. A daily prayer of mine is that I will be a leader of influence. I ask God for His favor in living out five characteristics of influence:

Influence Characteristic #1: Integrity. This word has many different definitions. I see integrity as a "condition" of one's personality that results from living out a number of character traits. Here are just a few:

- *Honesty*: I can rely on a person of integrity to tell me the truth—the complete truth, with discretion and with candor. An honest person uses good judgment about what to say, and when and how to say it. This person is careful to find the balance between saying too much and saying too little.
- *Authenticity*: The quality of being consistent in character and personality. The authentic person is a person of high character who is the same at work, at home, in the grocery store, at the ball field, etc. You know *where* an authentic person is coming from because you know *who* that person really is. Authentic people wear no masks.

■ **The authentic person is a person of high character who is consistently the same person. You always know where an authentic person is coming from because you know who they really are.**

- *Commitment*: Persons of integrity *say what they mean,* and they *mean what they say.* They will also *do what they say they will do.* They are dependable, and you never have to worry about the job getting done. If something comes up and they can't carry out their responsibility, they will see to it that it will get done.

■ **Persons of integrity say what they mean, and they mean what they say. They will also do what they say they will do.**

Influence Characteristic #2: Intentionality. People with intentionality live life on purpose. They are much more interested in controlling their circumstances than in letting their circumstances control them. They are proactive in the way they approach life, rather than being reactive. Therefore, they are much less likely to get caught up in circumstances out of their control. People who live life with intentionality are secure in their identity. They have confidence in their ability to make decisions about life. They are not afraid to fail. They know that sometimes they will make the wrong decisions and that consequences may be significant. But they are willing to take mistakes and turn them into lessons. They are persistent, and won't let those failures keep them from trying again. They see failure as a part of the journey to success, applying the lessons so that next time they will have a better chance to succeed.

■ **People who live life with intentionality are secure in their identity. They have confidence in their ability to make decisions about life. They are not afraid to fail.**

Influence Characteristic #3: Initiative. I once listened to a very well-respected leader—also a friend of mine—lead a seminar for church leaders. He talked about three things people need to be successful in the workplace, church, etc.: knowledge, skills, and resources. His presentation was great, but I felt a piece missing. I tried to figure out what it was. Finally, it hit me. A fourth element is needed for success—initiative. I made the point to my friend that someone can have knowledge, skills, and resources, but without the inner drive to make use of them, knowledge, skills, and resources may lie dormant—perhaps never to be used productively. Initiative is that inner drive that causes someone to "just do it," as the Nike slogan says. People of initiative don't wait around to be told to do something. They see a need and jump on it. Some of the people I admire the most are those who just seem to know what to do. Unfortunately, these people are few and far between.

■ **People of initiative don't wait around to be told to do something. They see a need and jump on it.**

Influence Characteristic #4: Intensity. People of intensity approach life with great energy. Living out of a life of purpose, people of intensity go all out. They give maximum effort in whatever they find worthwhile to do. People of intensity are focused. They keep their eyes on the goal—the objective. Perhaps one of the most intense people who ever lived was the apostle Paul. I love his words in Philippians 3:12–14:

> I don't mean to say that I have already achieved these things or that I have already reached perfection. But I press on to possess that perfection for which Christ Jesus first possessed me. No, dear brothers and sisters, I have not achieved it, but I focus on this one thing: Forgetting the past and looking forward to what lies ahead, I press on to reach the end of the race and receive the heavenly prize for which God, through Christ Jesus, is calling us.

■ **People of intensity go all out. They give maximum effort in whatever they find worthwhile to do.**

Influence Characteristic #5: Innovation. The leader must be willing to do new things. Innovation is about an open-mindedness that encourages looking for new solutions to old and new problems. Innovation is also the ability to keep an eye out for what is going on, and to see new possibilities for getting things done. People of innovation are unlikely to get stuck in doing the same things the same way. They also are able to influence others to think in terms of innovation and to try new things as well. The idea of efficiency—doing things the right way—is very important to people of innovation. They are often relentless in trying to get the most out of a process or situation, while using the least resources possible.

■ **Innovation is about an open-mindedness that encourages looking for new solutions to old and new problems.**

Although I only encountered Steve that day in the seminar, my hunch is that Steve regularly demonstrated these characteristics. He was truly a leader of influence among his people.

Realistic Expectations

Many leadership-deficient pastors staff positions in churches. On the other hand, many churches place unrealistic expectations upon the pastor. They expect the pastor to do everything and to be good at everything. This is often characteristic of the *hired hand* view of the pastor that we brought up earlier. The pastor is hired to do all of the ministry. These churches are typically very focused on themselves. They want someone to take care of them. They ignore the fact that much of the New Testament was written to describe how the church is to operate—with everyone joining in to do the ministry, based on their unique equipping by the Holy Spirit.

■ While there are many leadership-deficient pastors staffing positions in churches, there are also many churches that place unrealistic expectations upon the pastor.

Steve, though, didn't have to deal with unrealistic expectations. Over the years, he won over his church, gaining their respect through his ability to exhibit character traits that made him so easy to follow, and in focusing on what he was good at.

Leadership Continuity

I had never been around Steve to see him exercise leadership in the direct context of his congregation, but I did notice the leadership he exercised that day in the session. Steve had obviously built his leadership credibility over the course of his long tenure with the congregation. He had stuck with them through some pretty tough times—changes in senior pastoral leadership, controversy with folks leaving when the church tried some incremental changes in worship style or infrastructure, and, most recently, the fire and its affects on the congregation. Steve's longevity, along with all the other characteristics that Steve possessed, made him an easy person to follow.

One of the greatest enablers for good organizational health— church, business, etc.—is extended tenure among quality senior leadership. Good consistent leadership is required over long periods of time for an organization to become truly healthy. Unfortunately, churches have to deal with the issue of instability almost as a way of life. For the most part, pastors come and go, often looking for the next step on the *corporate ladder of the pastorate*. This movement often legitimately results from the movement of God in their lives. But often God's name is used to legitimize the pastor doing what he or she wants to do anyway.

■ In order to maximize their effectiveness, organizations must be very careful to find the right leaders, and to do all they can to keep them in leadership over the long haul.

To maximize their effectiveness, organizations must be very careful to find the right leaders and to do all they can to keep them in leadership over the long haul. All too often, each change at the top of any organization leads to starting all over again with new initiatives, new direction, etc.

Pulling It Together

A position at the top of the organization chart, whether it be a CEO, a store manager, a pastor, a coach, etc., doesn't make that person a leader. Rather, leadership flows out of a number of factors that really have nothing to do with the position held by the leader.

To move the organization forward, a leader must have credibility among the people of the organization. The people of the organization must want to follow. The leader must match up well with the people, so that they will be responsive. The leader must exercise real influence. The organization must have high, but realistic, expectations that match up with who the leader is. Finally, the leader must be willing to stick around to see initiatives through and to help the organization build long-term health.

Without strong, consistent, credible leadership, an organization will likely not be able to undertake effectively the *4D* process, or any planning process, for that matter.

The 4D Paradigm
Staffing and Other Key Considerations

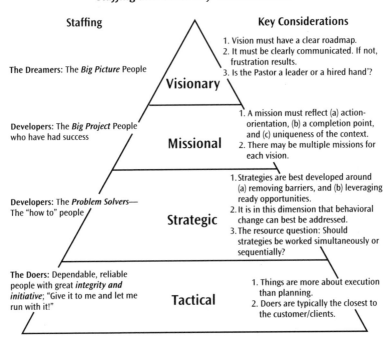

Staffing

Key Considerations

Visionary

The Dreamers: The *Big Picture* People

1. Vision must have a clear roadmap.
2. It must be clearly communicated. If not, frustration results.
3. Is the Pastor a leader or a hired hand'?

Missional

Developers: The *Big Project* People who have had success

1. A mission must reflect (a) action-orientation, (b) a completion point, and (c) uniqueness of the context.
2. There may be multiple missions for each vision.

Strategic

Developers: The *Problem Solvers*— The "how to" people

1. Strategies are best developed around (a) removing barriers, and (b) leveraging ready opportunities.
2. It is in this dimension that behavioral change can best be addressed.
3. The resource question: Should strategies be worked simultaneously or sequentially?

Tactical

The Doers: Dependable, reliable people with great *integrity and initiative*; "Give it to me and let me run with it!"

1. Things are more about execution than planning.
2. Doers are typically the closest to the customer/clients.

The Four Dimensions of Planning

9

Where Do We Start?

A popular spoof on psychiatry typically shows a therapist encouraging the patient to "start at the beginning" with the source of the patient's issues. The patient then proceeds to say something such as, "Well I was born thirty-seven years ago in a little town..." While this is not what the therapist was looking for, the patient took the request at face value and gave the answer the therapist asked for. The obvious place to start is—well, at the beginning! That is, in most cases. Many times, though, that it is not possible, and sometimes it is not very wise.

With the 4D process, the starting point is, of course, the vision. But, as we discussed earlier, a vision usually comes over time, with experience, and with the development of a better understanding of the organization's context. What happens when a church, or any organization, for that matter, wants to get moving on a planning process—but doesn't have that vision as a starting point? Should it wait until the vision becomes obvious? Should it try to rush the process of developing a vision, and then start?

An organization deciding it wants to kick off the 4D planning process will find that it's not as simple as coming up with a vision, working the mission, developing strategies, and then figuring the day-to-day tactical stuff. It is much more complex than that. Our church discovered this a few years ago.

An Integrity Church Story

When our church started back in 1997, we pretty much knew what we wanted to see happen in our town. Sensing God's call to vocational ministry, I had come out of a rewarding ten-year career in the corporate world and had been a youth pastor for the previous three and half years. I had been able to assemble a dynamite youth ministry volunteer team, and their leadership carried the ministry to a level of quality that it had never experienced before. Early in the fourth year of our ministry there, we decided to try a different approach: We would start a Sunday night teen service geared toward reaching kids in our community who were not in church. We decided that more edgy music would be appropriate, and we would meet in the church gym, while the traditional Sunday evening service was going on in the church worship center.

Needless to say, with the team I had around me, this was not really a difficult task. They came together beautifully and made it happen. The Sunday night teen service was a huge success in the context of our teen ministry. In our relatively small town, no one else was doing anything like this. So we had pretty much a captive audience. Most importantly, it brought in kids who would not come into our church on Sunday mornings.

The service went on regularly on Sunday evenings, having significant impact, for a few months. Then someone in the regular Sunday evening service (in the main worship center) looked around and asked, "Where are all the teens and teen 'leaders'?" The answer came, "They're out in the gym doing a teen 'contemporary' service." Before I realized what had happened, the Sr. Pastor, who had been so supportive of our venture, called me in to his office and told me to shut down the Sunday evening teen service. Never mind that the adult service in the worship center was not designed at all to appeal to teens. We had to shut it down, and we did.

Catalyzing a "New Idea"

While the experience with the Sunday night teen service was somewhat bittersweet, we took a lot from the experience. Our adult teen ministry leaders caught a glimpse of *something that could be* in our town, and not just for teenagers. On one of those Sunday evenings, after we had shut down the teen service, we went out to eat (a favorite Sunday evening routine) at a local hangout. One of the teen leaders, Kevin, came to me and said, "After seeing what God did with the teen service, we feel like He's telling us to start something new in our town—a church for families modeled after our teen service—and we feel like He's telling us to ask you to lead it!"

Now, my adult team consisted of the kind of folks who would run through a brick wall in the name of effective and impacting ministry. However, this one caught me by surprise. About a year earlier, I had picked up a book called *The Purpose Driven Church* by Rick Warren. Like millions who have read it, I was captivated. I remember thinking, "Why don't we all do church this way?" and "Why aren't churches in our area doing this?" I asked all of my adult team to read the book. Like me, they were blown away!

Over the previous year or so, I had come to realize that for me to grow as a leader and to be challenged on a regular basis, I would probably need a change of scenery in my own vocational ministry context. The church's decision to can the Sunday night teen service made it pretty obvious that a change was right for my family and me. So I had begun looking at the possibility of moving on to another church in a senior pastor role myself. I was even interviewed at a fairly sizable church in our area. However, none of that worked, as I couldn't find a fit. Nobody was really doing church any differently than we were already doing.

So, while I was surprised that my friend would bring up the idea of starting a new church and was certainly flattered that he would ask me to lead it, I was in fact ready for something new. I replied to him, "OK, let me pray about it." (By the way, that is always the super-spiritual answer to use when you don't know how to respond at the moment.) So, I prayed about it, and about ten seconds later, I said, "*OK, let's do it!*"

The Journey Begins

We agreed with each other that we would begin immediately planning for a new church to be launched in the next nine months or so. We also had a two-week teen mission trip coming up, and so we spent the bulk of our free time on that trip working together and planning for the new church launch. The *Purpose Driven Church* book became our "second Bible," and we were off to the races! We planned for the launch, even though we weren't quite sure when it would happen. Our church even gave us its blessing. When we rolled out our plans to them, they agreed to support us financially. Today, I like to joke that they gave us money to leave—probably a good move on their part!

Our planning was packaged in a book we called *"The Master Plan."* It was actually quite an impressive document. We included our vision, our mission, our philosophy of ministry, as well as lots of specific information about things we could in no way yet know about. But it was impressive! Our "vision" was built around the five biblical purposes in the Purpose Driven Model. Good stuff!

Years of Growing

The first couple of years in our church were great. Despite being quite inexperienced and having made numerous questionable decisions, we saw a great deal of growth. Like many new church starts, we met in a hotel for the first fifteen months or so, until we outgrew it. We endured the weekly Sunday morning *"haul it in before the service, and haul it out after the service"* routine. We then moved into an outlet mall building, which we would ultimately purchase and which serves as our home today.

■ **Timing is a real key to success.**

Times were good in those first two years. We modeled our services after the upbeat, casual, and always unpredictable nature of the Sunday night teen service we had done at our previous church. We continued to grow. People seemed to genuinely love each other, and we all enjoyed being together. New folks came regularly and stayed for the most part. As I look back now and try to analyze how things went so well in those first two years, two factors come to mind. First, we *simply received God's favor*. It seems that for nearly every one of our lemons, God made lemonade out of them. Second, I believe that *timing is a real key to success*. We were told that we were simply the first new church start that had come about in our town in the past twenty-five years or so that hadn't come out of a church split. So we were, in effect, the only ones in our town doing what we would call "contemporary church." When you're the only game in town, you have to mess it up pretty badly not to be successful. So—*God used timing in our situation*.

Growing Pains

Then the third year came. Everything continued to do well during the first few months. Then it hit—one of my secretaries, along with a couple of laypeople, told me about some "chatter" they had picked up among some of the more influential members. It turned out that they were some of those disgruntled churchgoers that had come from other area churches—*with their baggage*. When we looked a little deeper, we found that these influential members had been, in effect, plotting a coup, hoping to remove me from leadership and to take the church down a different road. They communicated their platform as a theological issue, when it was really based on their desire to control what was going on by assuming leadership of the church.

Fortunately, a strong group of elders handled the situation very well over the course of a number of months. Still, significant damage had been done. We lost all those folks who had been a part of the plot, including some of the founding group. Those folks, needless to say, needed to leave. But a number of other families, on the periphery of what had been going on, also left. Many of these represented ministry leaders and workers who had invested significant time and energy in our church. It hurt badly!

Losing this many families left us with a huge gap in ministry and ministry leadership, as well as in the budget. We had to act quickly to make adjustments, and ultimately we did. However, things were really tough. I remember standing in front of our church body (what was left of it) at a Sunday night meeting and telling the folks that I felt like our church had lost its innocence.

Brighter Days?

The next year things began to get a little brighter. We began seeing people step up into leadership roles. Attendance levels began to rise, and people were getting connected with each other. On the surface, things were looking like we had recovered pretty quickly. However, something very intangible was happening. Though God did some pretty cool stuff in putting our church back together, we really didn't do our part. This "crash," as I like to call it, robbed us of our "edge," our ability and willingness to take risks, to step out and try some unusual things. It's almost as if, as a defense mechanism, we pulled back, allowing caution to override innovation. We took on a "play it safe" posture. To be honest, it felt good because it felt, well, safe!

■ **This "crash," as I call it, robbed us of our "edge," our ability and willingness to take risks, to step out and try some unusual things.**

Forcing the Vision

Not until we had entered our sixth year or so did I realize what had happened. The effects of the crash and the recovery period were more extensive than we realized. We had lost our sense of vision. We had lost our willingness to be truly innovative, in trying new things. In an earlier discussion on missional planning, I mentioned that we put together a mission statement that turned out to be more of a purpose statement, and it failed to inspire our folks. We were lost.

During this time I learned a few things.

We were drifting as a church. I struggled with the question of, "What do we do next?" Very little really felt right. We shared no clarity. Earlier in this book, we said this about vision: "The organization must have a compelling picture that depicts *what could be*, and *what should be*, in the organization's future. Vision addresses the question, *'Where are we going?'"*

When it finally hit me, it hit me hard. We simply didn't have a vision. God had not downloaded that picture that we needed to move forward with intentionality. I had to ask the question, "What about the vision we had when we started the church?" Looking at that vision statement made it clear that the statement was simply a play on the five biblical purposes from the book *The Purpose Driven Church.* We made some of the same mistakes many churches had made. We had *forced a vision!*

■ **One of the reasons God gives vision over time is that it is very difficult for people to gain an understanding of a context until they have lived in that context for a while.**

As we discussed in chapter 3, when God gives a vision, He usually does it over a period of time. The vision comes as a result of experiences that come out of working in *a context,* whatever that may look like. One of the reasons God gives vision over time is that it is very difficult for people to gain an understanding of a context until they have lived in that context for a while. While living in that context, God typically uses those experiences to prepare us to receive what He wants us to see. We had been living off a vision—or what we thought was a vision—that we had when we started the church. Now the realization came: *It was not a vision after all, mainly because it had nothing to do with our context.* We did, however, have *a sense of vision* during that time.

Here's that first lesson we learned: Having *a sense of vision* differs from having *a true Vision.*

We had, from the beginning of the church, a very strong sense of vision, but not a true Vision. (To help distinguish these terms, in the following discussion we will capitalize the "V" when talking about a true Vision—a specific vision from God that fits the definition above and in chapter 3.) When we started our church, we knew the town in which we would operate and the area of town in which we would physically meet. We knew the people who had come together to start our church, and we had described a demographic group that we would target. But we could not see into the future to get a feel for what our future congregational demographic would look like. While we knew we would be starting our church in a hotel convention center, we recognized that as a temporary home. We couldn't visualize the physical structures in which we would one day meet. Finally, the leader of the group—yours truly—had never served as the lead pastor of a church. *So* we really had no idea how that leadership would play out. In many ways, our start-up team entered this venture with the blind leading the blind!

■ **There is a difference between having a sense of vision and having a true Vision.**

What we did have, though, was an energy, an enthusiasm, about what God would ultimately accomplish through the ministry of our church. We had our eyes on the Great Commandment in Matthew 22 and the Great Commission in Matthew 28. We truly loved each other and were willing to run through a brick wall together. We had a desire to be a catalytic force for spiritual growth in our community. We had a better feel for *what we wanted to do* than for *how our church would ultimately look*. In short, in the beginning of our church we never had a Vision in the sense of a clear picture from God, but we had a strong sense of vision.

This sense of vision is characterized by the attributes I just described about our start team. A sense of vision is more about *having a desire to receive a vision* from God. It is almost an emotional thing. Looking at Nehemiah and the development of his vision, in chapter 3 we noted that he spent lots of time laboring emotionally over the broken-down condition of the city of Jerusalem. We read of his agony, his tears, and the extent of his burden, which would cause him to make an almost unprecedented request of his boss, the king.

■ **A sense of vision is more about having a desire to receive a Vision from God... A sense of vision is usually built around the sensing of a need arising out of a problem, while a true Vision is built around a true solution to that need or problem.**

A sense of vision is usually built around the sensing of a need arising out of a problem, while a true Vision is built around a true solution to that need or problem. In the case of Nehemiah, for example, his burden led to a sense of vision, but it wasn't until he got to Jerusalem, surveyed the physical condition, the political climate, and the people that the Vision of a rebuilt city began to take shape.

Settling for a Sense of Vision

Is a leader deficient if all he or she has is *a sense of vision*, as opposed to a true Vision—a compelling picture of what could be, and should be? Absolutely not! It is important that the leader know the difference between the two. Therein lies the second lesson we learned: *distinguishing between having a sense of vision and having a true Vision is often difficult.*

■ **It is often difficult to distinguish between having a sense of vision and having a true Vision.**

As the director of an organization that focuses on helping pastors with leadership development issues, I talk to church planters, new pastors, and experienced pastors who are new to their churches. A common rallying cry for them may sound something like this: "I have a vision for this city coming to faith in Jesus Christ!" That is a great statement! It speaks to the heart of the leader, the enthusiasm of the pastor, and the intent of the pastor to work toward building the Kingdom of God in that town. But, in reality, the statement addresses the pastor's sense of vision and not a true Vision. It says a lot about what the pastor wants to happen. It says little about the church itself and less about the uniqueness of the geographic area. In short, it doesn't speak to the *context* of the church.

The difference between having a sense of vision and having a true Vision may be very subtle, but it is critical. A leader who tries to move forward while mistaking a sense of vision for a true Vision will likely only frustrate followers. As we said in chapter 4, vision is overrated without a clear path on which to move toward its fulfillment. "Vision can overwhelm people—the very people it is intended to inspire—when it is not accompanied by a 'roadmap' for the vision to be realized."

A leader who moves forward while mistaking a sense of vision for a true Vision from God will be able to move his organization forward for a good while, particularly while a freshness emanates from the energy of that sense of vision. Yet without the clear picture of a true Vision, real direction for followers will be limited. It may be difficult to develop solid missional plans, and then, strategic plans. Followers may become frustrated and stop working. They may even quit the church altogether.

It Takes Energy to Maintain the Energy

The third thing we learned from the experience of our crash and the effects of the crash was this: *a leader with a sense of vision,*

but not a true Vision, must work hard just to sustain that sense of vision.
A sense of vision is usually built around emotional aspects of
someone's makeup—i.e., enthusiasm, energy, desire for change,
for great things. A true Vision, on the other hand, will bring real
clarity. Clear communication makes it easier for followers to get
their arms around the Vision.

■   **Even if a leader has a sense of vision, and not a true Vision, the
leader must work hard to just sustain that sense of vision.**

Because a sense of vision often comes from an emotional
position, it will be more difficult to sustain. Emotions, by nature,
tend to shift over time, often with change in environmental
circumstances. Likewise, in an organization, followers affected
by a strong sense of vision from their leadership will find that
their energy, enthusiasm, etc., will likely ebb and flow according
to conditions within the organization and in the organization's
environment.

The Prerequisite to True Vision

We face the temptation to assume that having a sense of vision
is a negative alternative to having a True Vision. Nothing could be
further from the truth. In most cases, the visionary leader needs
a sense of vision before having the capacity to receive, or even
understand, a true Vision that comes from God. The key is for the
leader to know when they have a *sense of vision* and when they
have received a true Vision.

■   **The visionary leader needs a sense of vision before having the
capacity to receive, or even understand, a true Vision that comes
from God.**

An organization in a "pre-Vision stage" finds it important for
leadership to be honest with their followers about the wait for
Vision. I learned this the hard way. During that period between our
crash and the subsequent time of recovery, I tried to act as if we
had a clear Vision. I basically ignored the fact that we really didn't.
I seemed to rationalize the situation by thinking, *"I'm a visionary
thinker, so surely the Vision we had when we started (which was really
a sense of vision all along) can and will still carry us."* After a time of
trying to grab hold of a true Vision, my question became, *"I am a
visionary thinker, aren't I? Then why can't I ascertain God's Vision for
our church, and articulate it?"*

Finally, I had to admit that the vision we had when we started the church was no longer carrying us, partially because, as I know now, it was not a true Vision in the first place. Rather it was a legitimate *sense of vision*. At this point I had to confess, "*I don't have a Vision for our church. God just simply hasn't given me one for our church at this point.*" Making this statement publicly was one of the more freeing moments in the life of our church. While I had lost some of my confidence in my identity as a visionary thinker, their responses showed clearly that our congregation still trusted me as a visionary leader.

At this point in the life of our church, roughly seven years in, I realized that, despite not having a true Vision, we needed to move forward. We had been stagnant for a few years, and we needed some new direction. We needed the energy and enthusiasm that we once had. Because of the initial crash three years into our church, our congregation had turned over and looked quite different from the "pre-crash" days. To top things off, in the seventh year of our church, we had our second major crash, over a personnel issue. Again, we lost a significant proportion of our congregation—perhaps 40 percent, including a large number of leaders, even elders. In some ways, our congregation had turned over again—a second time. This situation made it more imperative that we move forward into a new direction. We had a new group of people—in effect, a new church.

So, we had a few "givens" in our situation. First, we now were working with, in effect, our third congregation in seven or eight years of our church's existence. Second, we had been drifting for a number of years with no clear direction. Third, the church's "visionary" lead pastor (again—yours truly) had been dry of vision for quite some time. Fourth, we had to move forward, in spite of the fact that we didn't have a true Vision before us.

It was this fourth 'given' that began to get my attention.

Figuring Out the Starting Point

Knowing we needed to move forward in spite of no true Vision, we concluded that the place to start planning for the future would be our *points of competency*. Each of our five ministry staff professionals—our pastoral staff—would focus on what was already being done well in his or her organization. We would develop initiatives around getting better in areas in which we were already performing reasonably well. We realized that this would also be a good training experience for our staff members, who were young and relatively inexperienced.

I started teaching the staff members to develop missional and strategic plans, focused on what would need to be done in their organizations over the next two to three years. Over the course of a couple of months, our staff members had done some good work. The plans were fully developed and ready to be introduced to those on their ministry teams.

■ **In spite of no true Vision, we came to the conclusion that the place to start planning for the future would be our points of competency.**

The next step was the rollout to the ministry teams. At the beginning of the year we gathered as many of the leaders as we could in what we called a strategic planning retreat. We invited all our folks who worked in ministry areas—Dreamers, Developers, and Doers. We wanted to expose as many people as possible to the process. Our turnout for the retreat was actually very good. I laid out the agenda for the two-day event and went through the history, year by year, of our church. Then each staff ministry leader and the particular ministry team went into session with a hired external coach/facilitator.

The role of the coach/facilitator was to lead the group sessions, freeing the staff ministry leader to participate as one of the team members (more on this later). The main objective of the two-day session was for the ministry teams to work together to develop strategic plans for the teams to pursue over the next one to two years. The results of the event were very encouraging. Four of the five groups came up with very thorough strategic plans. Their teams were energized, and each of the four went right to work when the retreat was over. Ultimately these four groups found great success, working through their plans, with three of them actually completing their work ahead of schedule.

The True Vision

During the planning for the strategic planning retreat, God's Vision for our church began to come into focus. Over the course of a couple of years, our church had time to further develop that Vision. As we were ready to move into the 4D process, our people had a chance to become familiar with the Vision that God has downloaded, and they have had an opportunity to become familiar with the planning process.

I really wish I could say that this whole thing worked out because of the great wisdom and savvy of our church's lead pastor. Actually, this was something we "backed into." So, our learnings just "evolved" as we took some action steps to move forward in absence of a true Vision. Again, we felt we had to get moving. So we did. Here are just four of those learnings:

Don't Rush the Vision

A Vision is a *huge* thing! The development of a Vision can't be rushed. My wife is a fabulous cook. She learned well from her mom, also one of the best. When I, or one of my kids, want something to eat, we will often put leftovers or a frozen dinner into the microwave. The snack or meal will likely be just fine—particularly leftovers from one of my wife's meals. But when I walk in to the house and smell the crock pot going in the kitchen, I know it's going to be really good! It will most likely be a very special meal. Development of a Vision is so much more like a crock pot process than a microwave meal. The longer the process, the more clarity the Vision is likely to have. A congregation, for example, must allow the process of receiving a Vision from God to run its course. It takes time, as we said earlier, for the organization to develop a context. Once that context is developed, the context can shift, often dramatically. Even minor shifts in urban, suburban, and rural demographics will often have major implications for congregations. To rush the process could give the congregation a counterfeit vision, and thus a false starting point. A false starting point, one that is not reflective of where the organization should be headed, will likely render the entire planning process useless, wasting time and resources in pursuit of the wrong vision. When our church didn't have a true Vision from God and realized it, we sensed the temptation to rush it. Ultimately we resisted that temptation.

■ **Development of a vision is so much more like a crock pot process than a microwave meal. The longer the process, the more clarity the vision is likely to have.**

Act Quickly to Start the Process

As soon as an organization realizes it has hit a point of stagnation resulting from a perceived lack of direction, it should move rapidly to initiate a fresh planning process. It is potentially dangerous to let the organization drift along, without clear vision. The longer this condition is allowed to linger, the longer it will likely take to pull out of it. In all organizations, good habits take quite a while to develop, but bad habits seem to come a little more quickly. I wish our church had moved more quickly when it became apparent that we needed to move forward, even without the true Vision. Because we didn't detect the need to begin a new planning process, we had to spend a good bit of time digging out of a hole that we dug in the first place.

■   **It is potentially dangerous to let the organization drift along, without clear vision.**

Start Where You're Strong

When you have no true Vision from which to begin the planning process, the organization should look to start with missional, strategic, and/or tactical planning around its areas of strength. This will help ensure success and will build positive momentum toward the time when the organization's Vision is clear. Research has indicated that an individual will be more productive on the whole by trying to get better in areas of competency rather than in areas of weakness. The same is true of an organization, simply because the organization is made up of those individuals. Focusing on strengths will afford a greater likelihood of success, simply because the organization has already established those competencies at some level. Successes will tend to motivate those in the organization, and continued successes will further motivate them. One of the really good things we did in trying to move forward was to determine these areas of competency for each of the ministry areas and to develop missional and strategic plans around them. We were able to experience significant successes in a relatively short period of time. The result has been a higher confidence level, I believe, among our ministry staff and leaders. They are simply much better prepared to handle a planning process that originates with true Vision and to see it through.

■   **Focusing on strengths will afford a greater likelihood of success, simply because the organization has already established those competencies at some level.**

Keep Going

At whatever dimension an organization begins the process in the absence of true Vision, it must continue sequentially in the process on through the tactical dimension. The movement from the big picture perspective toward the day-to-day operations in an organization is crucial. An organization that starts with missional planning can't then just jump to the visionary dimension, even if it senses that it has a true Vision. It will be best for this organization to continue in a sequential manner, into strategic, and then tactical, planning. For an organization to jump around in its order of planning would lead to a number of things:

1. Organizational morale may suffer as *members sense a lack of consistency and closure.* There is great value in finishing the job.
2. *To stop a planning process and start another could do real* damage in that members may miss an opportunity to experience the success that comes with a completed planning process and with the execution of those plans.
3. The organization may suffer from schizophrenia. If the planning process is not completed before another is begun, *organizational members may not know where to focus.* They may find the temptation to toggle back and forth between each of the processes.

■ **The movement from the big-picture perspective toward the day-to-day operations in an organization is crucial.**

Pulling It Together

Thinking of the levels of planning, we naturally begin with the vision. Real Vision should always be the starting point for an effective organizational planning process. However, an organization may find itself in a situation in which it doesn't have a true Vision. This may happen because the organization is new and still trying to get a handle on its organizational context and/ or its own organizational uniqueness. The organizational context may be in a significant state of transition, and the new "look" of the context will effectively alter the Vision. Perhaps the organization has been "adrift" without a clear vision for a long period of time, and leadership wants to begin forward movement.

A complicating factor is that many organizations are inherently unaware of the difference between *having a sense of vision,* which describes the desire and foresight to receive, understand, and articulate a specific organizational vision, and *having a true Vision,* which is that clear, compelling picture of what could be, and should be, in an organization's future.

Whatever the case, an organization without a true Vision needs to start somewhere to begin a trend of forward movement. Usually the best place to start, until the organization gets a sense of its true

Vision, is the development of missional and strategic planning around areas of strength, or its competencies. It is important to recognize this: *at whatever level an organization starts, it will be best to follow the planning dimensions in the order prescribed.* After all, vision forms the framework for mission, mission provides framework for strategy, and strategy forms a framework for the tactics. Having started the process, the organization should remain "on go" to give the members a sense of accomplishment and to avoid going off in several directions at once.

PART IV

Sustaining the 4D Paradigm

Successful organizations, including congregations, will seek to adopt the ideal of *continuous improvement as a way of life*. The idea of improvement being truly continuous in an organization is grounded in the realization that *the improvement process should be cyclical*. For that to happen, *continuous improvement must be deeply embedded* in the DNA of the organization.

In a truly innovative congregation, for example, every situation, every new day, will be approached with these questions in mind, "How can we make this process or program better?" and, "What can I do today to make it better?"

An environment of continuous improvement can be very empowering in a congregation. One of the biggest challenges congregational leadership will face is the issue of *driving ownership within the church's membership*. A true focus on continuous improvement can drive that ownership by putting the onus for determining what improvements are necessary on those who are closest to the operational, or tactical, level of execution. For example, what happens when a greeter is given the freedom to determine ways that the First Impressions Team can be better configured to provide quality touches for guests of the church? What if the greeter has the freedom to work with other team members to implement those changes, without having to go through bureaucratic channels? That greeter will likely take greater ownership, and more pride, in his or her work. He or she will more likely demonstrate dependability, excellence, and a willingness to continuously improve at what he or she already does.

Just as improvement should not be considered a single event, but rather a continuous pursuit, so implementing the *4D* planning process *should be considered a continuous pursuit*. After all, the right improvements should be planned for. *Healthy planning, simply put, will be continuous*, as it facilitates continuous improvement.

Continuous improvement won't happen without continuous planning. They simply go hand-in-hand.

■ **A true focus on continuous improvement, by nature, puts the onus for determining what improvements are necessary on those folks who are closest to the operational, or tactical, level of execution.**

When done effectively, continuous planning will facilitate continuous improvement which, will lead to a culture of continuous transition. This culture of continuous transition stems from the ideas that *planning must always be focused on generating improvement* in the organization, increasing the capacity of the organization to serve its clients, and that *improvement must be a constant pursuit, and so planning for that improvement must be a constant pursuit.*

■ **Continuous planning will facilitate continuous improvement, which will lead to a culture of continuous transition.**

In this section, we will discuss how to establish and sustain that culture of continuous improvement.

10

The Cyclical Nature of Planning

Sherrie Johnson started *Home Helps* out of her home eleven years ago. Although she didn't realize it, her home had been a testing ground, in many ways, for the development of the company. In her teenage years, she had been the picture of a person having a great ability to organize things. Her friends often picked at her because everything about Sherrie seemed to be so neat and in order. She always seemed to know where everything was and how to get to it.

Before having children, Sherrie had worked four years as a teacher in one of the local elementary schools. She and husband Eric had agreed, however, that once kids came along, she would stay at home with them, at least until they all went off to school. At that point, they figured she could restart her teaching career. With summers off, and a similar schedule with the kids, she would be able to spend lots of time with them.

With the birth of Matthew, five years into their marriage, right on the schedule that she and Eric had agreed on, Sherrie settled in nicely as a stay-at-home mom. She found that she had a fairly easy time with her new role. She had help from her mother, who lived just a few blocks away, and to help matters, Matthew was an easy child to care for. In addition, Sherrie's organizational skills benefited her even more in the home than they had in her teaching position. Their home seemed to run smoothly.

Two years later, another big blessing came along in the form of little sister Marie. Like Matthew, Marie turned out to be a fairly low maintenance child. Sherrie soon had developed a daily routine with the kids and realized she had more time on her hands than she ever thought she would. Always known among her friends and former teaching colleagues for her high energy and her high level of organizational skills, she began finding time to dabble in helping other moms—many of whom she had come in contact with through her church—with organizing their homes. She was amazed that so many of these mothers had so little time to work on their homes in terms of scheduling, physical appearance, storage of their stuff, and particularly basic personal financial management. After all, these things had come relatively easily to Sherrie.

As word got around about Sherrie's ability to help others with this rather tedious area of life, her phone began to ring constantly, despite never having marketed her services. Word about Sherrie was getting around! Sherrie enjoyed very much helping other folks with organizing their homes, as she understood and appreciated the freedom she experienced by having her own home organized.

Sherrie found her newfound hobby to be very rewarding. By the time she was working consistently with six other mothers, Eric approached her one evening and said, *"Sherrie, you really seem to be in a groove when you're working with another mother to get her home organized. How does that make you feel? And is this something you would like to do as a career? You just seem to be so happy when you're doing it."* She thanked Eric but didn't really respond. Instead she chose to think about it for a few weeks. Their next conversation on the subject somewhat surprised Eric as Sherrie told him that she would like to start a small business focused on the theme of home organization. Rather than her going back to teaching when Marie went to school, she would like to focus on building the home organization business. Sherrie's idea was that over the next three to four years, with her mom's willingness to help with Matthew and Marie, she could spend a significant amount of time developing the business.

Just two weeks after Marie's second birthday, Sherrie's new business, *Home Helps,* was formed. Sherrie found that with just a couple of newspaper advertisements and with flyers hung around the elementary school where she had taught, the phone calls came fast and furious. Most moms all around town seemed to be drowning in a sea of activity. Many of them lived lives that seemed to be out of control, as the convergence of the demands of their marriages, motherhood, home management, and careers brought symptoms of chaos. Sherrie was somewhat selective with the clients she took on in those first few years. She wanted to make sure she was not overloaded, as Matthew and Marie were still at home. However, the business grew steadily over the next three years. Even before Marie started school, Sherrie had already trained and hired two associates, both mothers she had worked with prior to starting the business. They had caught on and done very well with home organization.

Once Marie started school, Sherrie shifted the business into another gear. She began to take on a higher number of clients, and her associates were catching on well. She had made two very good decisions in hiring these ladies, as they all three seemed to have the same mindset about their work.

Over the next five years, the business grew at a clip that far exceeded Sherrie or Eric's expectations. The extent of their planning when the company originally got going was basically a mission statement that read…

Home Helps exists to help mothers get their homes under control, so that their homes don't control them.

Their idea was to establish long-standing relationships with their clients. They wanted to provide more than just "quick fixes." They planned to help mothers manage organizationally as they passed through different stages of their families' lives.

Five years after shifting the business into that next gear, with eleven associates working anywhere from 20–50 hours each week, Sherrie realized that the business was now beginning to control her. She had been so busy servicing clients herself over the past five years that she had lost focus on working with her associates and helping them be the best they could be. She had begun to notice an increase in "separations," as she called them, when clients would drop *Home Helps* services. She also saw the disappointment these separations were causing her associates. Productive hours for her associates dropped an average of 8 percent during year five alone. Sherrie knew she had to do something—and quick.

So, thanking God consistently for a mother—hers—who supported her totally and loved to help take care of her grandchildren, and encouraged by a husband who had continuously demonstrated a willingness to sacrifice to help Sherrie fulfill her dream, Sherrie decided to devote an additional twelve hours a week for the next three months to do some serious research. She would interview each of the twenty-seven clients that had separated in the past three years, and each of the other 119 current *Home Helps* clients. For the first time since starting the business, she was going to her clients to get at the answers to the questions that really mattered to her business: *"What's working and why?" "What's not working, and why?"* and, *"Where do we go from here?"*

Sherrie's three months of research yielded some fairly discouraging, yet valuable, information. A large number of *Home Helps* clients separated not because of any monumental dissatisfaction with the company's services. Rather, they felt that they didn't need the services of the company anymore. As a matter of fact, eighteen former clients cited that because *Home Helps* had helped them become more organized around their homes, they were now more interested in the whole home organization scene. As a result, they had done research on their own, and had found new products and services, ranging from cooking systems to personal financial management software to personal learning and tutoring aids for school age children. Unfortunately, fourteen of these clients had said that although these products and services clearly represented advances in home management, their *Home Helps* associates knew very little, if anything, about them. As a result, the credibility of the *Home Helps* associates had taken a hit. To make matters worse, because the business was one driven by word-of-mouth advertising among ladies who already knew each other, word of this situation spread rapidly among *Home Helps* clients.

Sherrie had to admit that she had never been consistent at requiring, or even encouraging, her associates to keep up with new opportunities, trends, products, and services in home organization services. She had to admit that even she was not familiar with many of the advances mentioned by the separated clients. Sherrie had to face the cold hard fact that *Home Helps* had not done a good job enhancing its abilities to serve its customers. They had become stale in this area. Sherrie knew they had much work to do.

A Cycle of Quality

Quality is important! That is probably one of the biggest "duuuuuhhhhh" statements ever made. Of course quality is important. Without high quality, a business, such as Sherrie's, will at some point find it impossible to compete. A church, for example, will find it difficult to attract, retain, and grow people.

Much of the corporate world in the 1980s and 1990s was characterized by a huge "quality movement." Industry, mostly in a positive way, became almost obsessed with the issue of quality. Measurement systems focusing on the *"quality of quality"* were developed. Many companies were able to utilize such measures to enhance their own market positions. Quality organizations sprang up and began to offer awards for companies who exhibited significant progress toward improving their quality. Fierce competition developed for coveted awards such as these.

In my own corporate environment, each organization was expected to follow strict guidelines and to provide staff members for teams, committees, etc., that would be focused on improving the overall quality of the division. We seemed to pull out all the stops to develop a culture of what was called *continuous improvement.* This culture would be driven by imbedded processes and systems designed to ensure a perpetual cycle of increasing quality. Again, all very good stuff. But because quality had become an "end in itself," we tended to get our focus off the end product. Ultimately, we found a better balance, with the idea of quality in its proper perspective.

■ **The emphasis on what we called "continuous improvement" really made its mark.**

As I look back on those days, I realize that the emphasis on quality was critical. It led to higher levels of efficiency, effectiveness, and, ultimately, employee and customer satisfaction. The emphasis on what we called "continuous improvement" really made its mark. This aspect of the quality movement was at the core of Edwards Deming's ideas about quality. Dr. Deming is known as "the father of the Japanese post-war industrial revival" and is seen by many as the all-time leading quality guru in the United States. The very first of Deming's "14 Points" leading to organizational transformation, called *Constancy of Purpose,* relates to this idea of continuous improvement:

> Create constancy of purpose for continual improvement of products and service to society, allocating resources to provide for long range needs rather than only short term profitability, with a plan to become competitive, to stay in business, and to provide jobs.[1]

Discrete Improvement

Most organizations truly desire to improve—most of them on a regular basis, whether in sporadic spurts, or in a cyclical or

---

[1]Edward Deming, as quoted in "Who Is Dr. W. Edwards Deming?" Leadership Institute, Inc. http://www.lii.net/deming.html.

continuous manner. However, a key question for any organization relates to the particular approach the organization adopts toward improvement.

In organizations characterized by this *sporadic spurt* approach to improvement, the idea of improvement is almost an afterthought—until a problem turns up, or perhaps results come in at lower-than-expected levels. Such an approach can be called *discrete* improvement. The *American Heritage Dictionary* defines the word *discrete* as "constituting a separate thing...[or] consisting of unconnected distinct parts." Further, in a mathematical context, the word refers to "a finite or countable set of values; not continuous."

In organizations using a discrete improvement approach, improvements do come in spurts. They usually have to be initiated by someone in the organization. The improvement process is usually an "event," bound by time frames. Often, once the improvement has been achieved, operations continue, and the idea of improvement only comes up again when results are below expectations.

■ **A discrete improvement process can contribute to perpetuating a status quo organization, in that things change only when there is a specific need for movement toward improvement.**

A discrete improvement process can contribute to perpetuating a *status quo organization,* in that things change only when there is a *specific need for movement toward improvement.* Once the need for improvement is perceived, and then developed and implemented, a new status quo is created, and the organization may continue on that new path until the next need for improvement arises. In a discrete improvement environment, *improvement initiatives will likely be expensive, as each will require start-up efforts and associated costs.*

Most congregations regularly operate in a discrete improvement mode. Often, a crisis of some sort drives the church to grasp the need for change. Once the change is addressed, the church operates with this new focus, until the next crisis arises.

Continuous Improvement

The 4D planning process should be used with the intent to drive a *culture of continuous transition.* An organization's culture is simply the sum total of the accepted, and expected, way of life within the organization. The culture is made up of a number of things, including the organization's corporate values, its beliefs about itself and the constituency it serves, and leadership and management style, to name just a few. It also incorporates factors such as whether the organization is bureaucratic or innovative in nature.

An innovative organization will respond rapidly to changes within its context, which include its internal climate and its external environment. Innovative organizations, then, are those that have developed the ability to "turn on a dime," as the saying goes, because *their cultures are built around doing what it takes to respond* to those contextual changes.

■　**The best prevention for falling into complacency is an intentional, proactive approach in creating that culture of continuous transition.**

An organization that wishes to drive a culture of continuous transition will have to work at it. Once it gets to a point of living that culture, the organization must also work hard to stay that way. The organization will always have to *resist the tendency to become complacent.*

The results of complacency can be disastrous. The best prevention for falling into complacency is to develop an intentional, proactive approach in creating that culture of continuous transition. *Planning for improvement must be established as an organizational priority, with position descriptions, schedules, and leadership assignments making room for continuous planning.* If continuous planning is promoted, emphasized, and demonstrated consistently, then continuous transition can become a way of life, and a new culture can be developed.

How can the 4D planning process help develop a culture of continuous transition?

Wrestling with Who We Are Today

The ideal beginning point for the 4D process is the vision for the organization. However, at some point early in the process, the organization must get an accurate picture of where it is today. It must also come to grips with its identity—its *current reality.* The organization must be honest about its current reality. The current reality establishes a baseline for the organization's improvement process. If the vision is a true Vision, one that truly reflects the *preferred future* of the organization, and if it captures the potential of the organization, it will highlight the gaps between that preferred future and the organization's current reality.

■ **If the vision is a true Vision, it will highlight the gaps between that preferred future and the organization's current reality.**

Self-analysis is not usually easy. Looking internally and objectively at the same time is difficult. If the current reality is not accurately defined, then everything else in the planning process is thrown off. For example, if the *stated vision doesn't reflect the proper direction* of the organization, then the *mission may not reflect the unique capabilities* of the organization. Then the *strategies may target barriers that don't really exist* in the organization's true context.

An organization's current reality depicts where it is at a given point in time. It is the general biographical information about the organization. The current reality is, in effect, *a story that portrays the identity of the church "as it is today."* The current reality encompasses things such as descriptions of organizational demographics, operational processes, major activities, assessments of organizational health, etc. Understanding the organization's current reality is key to identifying barriers to organizational change, and thus barriers to *continuous transition.*

Any process must be measured to determine whether it is successful. An understanding of the current reality serves as a *baseline* to help measure progress in the transitioning process. An inaccurate picture of the current reality could have devastating effects on the organization, leading to a distorted picture of the transitioning process. Just as a mother can get a feel for the body temperature of her child only by using a properly calibrated thermometer, *organizational leaders can get a proper feel for whether progress is being made only when their measurement incorporates the proper basis.*

The current reality in the organization can serve as a "baseline" against which progress can be measured. Once that current reality is defined, however, the most relevant points about that current reality must be brought into the light.

Defining the Gaps

When we earlier discussed the missional and strategic dimensions of planning, we noted that an organizational mission must be action-oriented, must have a completion point, and must be unique to the organization. Strategies, we said, must be synergistic with other strategies. Also, to determine which strategies an organization should pursue, it should identify the barriers that could keep the organization from meeting its mission, and ultimately the vision. Strategies, then, should be built around these barriers. Successful execution of the strategies would then enable successful completion of the mission, and thus would allow the vision to emerge.

To help determine areas of potential strategic initiative, the vision and missional thrusts of the organization must be compared with points about the organization's current reality. The differences between these constitute "gaps," which could represent the organization's *areas of strategic opportunity.*

■ **The differences between the vision and the current reality constitute "gaps," which could represent the organization's areas of strategic opportunity.**

A legitimate organizational Vision that stretches and challenges the organization will, by nature, identify many gaps. The results of this "gap analysis" can give valuable insight into the organization. A true Vision will challenge the organization. It will stretch its resources. Alleviating these gaps will require hard work and great attention to detail. A true Vision will reveal many of these gaps.

Gap Analysis and the Organization's Planning Horizon

An organization's visionary horizon typically lasts from seven to ten years. In fact, many would argue that given today's rapid rate of societal change, the visionary horizon may be as short as five to seven years. However, the *longer an organization has been living out a culture of continuous transition, the longer its visionary planning horizon may be.*

The organization that has just committed to a culture of continuous transition will have to get started with perhaps a relatively short-term planning horizon—one that may not require the organization to look too far into the future. By the same token, an organization that has been driven by vision, and has successfully worked through visionary cycles before, may try to look at a horizon of fifteen to twenty years, perhaps even further out.

Gap Analysis and Home Helps

Now, back to Sherrie and *Home Helps.* With the realization that she and her associates hadn't been doing a very good job of keeping up with new products and services that can be viable in home organization, Sherrie was determined to correct the problem. She really "got it"—understanding that her small company needed to develop a *culture of continuous transition,* so that they would never again be caught short in being able to meet the needs of the client. She committed to developing within *Home Helps* a culture of continuous transition, and was willing to work through a comprehensive planning process with her associates. A visionary thinker herself, Sherrie recognized that as a still-new business just starting out in the planning process, *Home Helps'* visionary horizon could not be very far-reaching. Since its commitment to continuous transition was new, the business adopted a vision that, Sherrie felt, took the organization five to six years into the future. She sensed that anything longer than that could overwhelm the associates and could serve to sabotage its efforts to build a new culture. A very high level summary of the three-page vision statement Sherrie wrote to be communicated to the associates says that *Home Helps* exists...

> To be a world-class company that enables the family to enjoy a higher quality home life through the use of home organization techniques, focusing on food selection and preparation, clutter prevention, room organization and cleanliness, and personal financial and investment management.

■ **An organization that has been driven by vision, and has successfully worked through visionary cycles before, may try to look at a horizon of 15–20 years, perhaps even further out.**

Sherrie and her team then developed two major missional thrusts that she thought would propel *Home Helps* toward fulfillment of that vision.

- *Missional Thrust 1:* Home Helps will double its market share over the next four years and will become one of the top five home organization consulting businesses in the state.
- *Missional Thrust 2:* Home Helps associates will serve their clients more effectively by staying on the cutting edge of opportunities and trends in home organization. They will be constantly and actively aware and knowledgeable of new opportunities, products, and services that may improve the quality of life in the homes of their clients.

Once Sherrie and her more senior level associates agreed on the visionary and missional direction for the business, they identified *nine key gaps*—at least five of them associated in some way with the lack of continuing education of their associates. Then Sherrie and her senior level associates worked on prioritizing the nine gaps. Their approach was to focus on those that, if addressed, would yield the most significant positive impact in moving the organization toward its vision.

Recognizing that resources could be stretched only so far, Sherrie chose to focus on three of these gaps, and to develop strategic initiatives around each of them. These three gaps, very simply stated, are summarized as follows:

1. To meet market share goals, we lack sufficient qualified associate level staff. To double our market share in four years, we will require a minimum of a 75 percent increase in the number of trained, full-time equivalent associates.
2. Fulfilling market share goals will require significant capital outlays toward advertising and promotion. A 125 percent increase in advertising investment will be required in the next year alone.
3. "Home organization technology" is rapidly advancing, but there are no easily accessible means of becoming aware of, and staying aware of, trends, products, and services. Home Helps must find new ways for associates to become aware of, and expert in, these new technologies as they emerge.

As these gaps were addressed through the development of the appropriate strategic initiatives, *Home Helps* began to experience some real successes, and ultimately the gaps began to close. After a year of working these gaps, Sherrie and her team re-analyzed the business's current reality and discovered that in the process of addressing those three gaps, an additional three of the nine gaps had been resolved, as a by-product of the work on the three primary gaps. Further, as the new current reality was updated and defined, two new gaps arose, both of which represented significant areas of opportunity for the organization.

Before too long, through consistent attention to detail and commitment to continuous transition, *Home Helps* saw its vision come to fruition and was ready to seek a new vision—one that would be even more challenging. As a result, *the process begins all over again*. Its visionary horizon from the earlier planning cycle, in which the organization chose to look five to six years out, has now been expanded in the second cycle of visionary planning, to eight to ten years.

The Cycle Continues

As the organization moves through its strategic plans, working on the gaps, or the barriers, it must constantly re-evaluate its current reality. That is because the current reality shifts with each completed strategy and each completed mission. The way the organization responds to shifts in its environment will change as well. The cycle continues as the organization moves out of one visionary planning cycle into another. The new cycle, then, brings a new vision, which will result in new missions, strategies, and tactical plans. The planning process, again, is so embedded in the DNA of the organization that it has become second nature. Truly *continuous transition results.*

> ■ **The current reality shifts with each completed strategy and each completed mission. The way the organization responds to shifts in its environment will change as well.**

As the organization continues to work successfully through planning cycles, its visionary horizon will expand. For example, *Home Helps* has been successful in a cycle based on a five-to-six-year horizon. Pursuing its next cycle, the company will likely look much further into the future.

Oft-Missing Ingredients

For an organization to develop a culture of continuous transition, perhaps the most important element is a *sustained commitment* to developing that very culture. The second critical element is *leadership continuity*. These two elements certainly feed off each other. For example, a commitment to a culture of continuous transition will not sustain unless those who staff leadership positions hold and demonstrate that commitment.

> ■ **One of the most frustrating things for any organization occurs when leadership changes bring philosophical changes.**

One of the most frustrating things for any organization occurs when leadership changes bring philosophical changes. I worked once with a particularly sizable division of a large organization that experienced such frustration. The organization was faced with a critical need to change direction quickly and decisively, and the success of this particular division would be key to the overall organization's success. The urgency of the need to change was quite obvious. Jobs and even careers were at stake, as was the very future of the organization.

As I spoke to the division employees, and in turn heard from them, I was shocked to see how resistant so many of them were. The division's leader had effectively laid out a vision that everyone had *seemed* to buy into. Yet as discussion continued and we went deeper into the shifts in responsibilities that might be required, the members made their resistance clear. I wondered what was really going on. The leader was well-respected. The team members loved him and actually seemed to appreciate his assertiveness in laying out his vision. They gave plenty of lip service to what he had said. However, I asked the team why so many of them seemed so reluctant to buy in to that vision. One influential member spoke up, "We had this very same conversation five years ago. We settled on a direction. Then that leader was moved. A new one came in, and the direction was changed. That has been the pattern for many, many years. We know that it will happen again."

Her answer revealed the real problem: *the organization had always had a short-term focus—starting at the top level of leadership.* They had never experienced a unified vision that the entire organization could rally around. Without a unified vision, they saw no attempt to establish a culture of continuous transition. As a result, direction of the organization shifted on an almost arbitrary basis.

Now, as the divisional leader was attempting to drive his vision, the team resisted. Not because of any dislike of, or disrespect for, the divisional leader, but because the employees simply didn't trust top leadership. The attitude was something like this: "Whatever direction he lays out for us, top management will change anyway, and the direction will also change."

> ■ **The organization's historically constant shifts in direction had taken their toll on the ability of the employees to trust top management.**

Again, the divisional leader was popular with his employees. They wanted to follow him. But the organization's historically constant shifts in direction had taken their toll on the ability of the employees to trust top management.This lack of trust, again, is but a symptom of those two much deeper problems: a) the lack of a sustained commitment to developing a culture of continuous transition, and b) a very superficial commitment to a philosophy of leadership continuity.

Pulling It Together

Healthy organizations will seek to make ongoing planning a high priority. They will seek to build *cultures of continuous transition.* This culture is fostered by a pursuit of continuous planning that leads to continuous improvement.

An organization's culture is simply the accepted way of life within the organization. The culture incorporates the values, its beliefs about the organization and the constituency it serves, and its philosophies of leadership and management. A natural outgrowth of the planning process is the recognition of deficiencies and gaps between where a congregation wants to be (the vision), and where it is today. Effective strategic and tactical plans will address these gaps. As a result, new pictures of the future will emerge. Usually, then, a healthy planning process will bring out "tweaks" that should be made in the vision and mission of the congregation. The vision then becomes a dynamic picture that evolves as changes in the environment come to light.

In healthy organizations, the planning process "cycles." As the organization approaches the realization of the stated vision, it will seek to develop a new vision and will move forward with the missional, strategic, and tactical dimensions of planning, based on that new vision. This cycle continues, and the result will ultimately be the establishment of that culture of continuous transition.

11

Keeping the Periscope above the Water Level

As a kid I loved to watch old war movies. The submarines that patrolled the deep and combated the opposing naval fleet deeply intrigued me. I think my favorite thing about those submarines was the periscope—an incredibly useful tool that would allow the captain of the sub a much better look at what was going on in the world far above the sub itself.

In the movies, the submarine captains who used their periscopes effectively would find new targets to engage and would help move the U.S. Navy toward victory. On the other hand, those who failed to use the periscope properly missed out on opportunities that may have been sighted only through the visibility the periscope made possible.

The Visionary Leader's Periscope

Visionary leaders have natural built-in periscopes. They have the ability to see beyond where the organization is at a given point in time and can usually provide direction that will carry the organization and its crew toward the right destination. *The best visionary leaders have their periscopes up at all times.* They are constantly on the lookout for opportunities that will grow the organization in a healthy manner. But what happens when visionary leaders fail to keep those periscopes raised? Simply put, the organizations they lead will suffer. To illustrate this, let's look at Nate. Nate's story is built around his experiences as a new church starter. However, what Nate experienced can easily occur in any organization in which a visionary leader rises to the occasion to craft and communicate a vision. It can happen in *any new business or church*. It can also happen in a business or church that *begins an intentional process of transition*.

Nate's Story

Nate grew up in a family that stressed positive values and strong morality. While his family went to church regularly at the local chapel, he never heard his parents talk much about spiritual issues. His dad would hammer home the values of honesty, integrity, and hard work. But Nate remembered no serious impact by anything said at the chapel. The pastors (all five or six of them) quoted from the Bible but just as easily from popular current "pop psychological" authors. Even now he wonders just how many people the ministry of the little chapel affected positively down through the years.

All through his childhood and teen years, Nate became known as a big dreamer. His vivid imagination evoked all kinds of kidding, mostly good-natured. At the same time, Nate knew he had developed as a good listener. He had always enjoyed people and having fun with them. Nate never had a shortage of friends. To satisfy his insistent and persistent roommate, Nate attended an on-campus Bible study during his freshman year in college. He didn't feel the study would be of any benefit but went anyway. He went back a second time after the teaching on the Gospel of John grabbed him. He realized he was hearing things he had never heard at the little chapel. Before long, Nate was a regular at the study. By the time he had been going for nine months, he had actually substituted for the leader a couple of times.

Nate began to understand that Christianity was a lifestyle and not just a religion. The message transformed his way of thinking. Much of what the little chapel taught, he realized, was contrary to what the Bible said. This just made him a more eager student. What he was hearing now simply made sense! By Nate's senior year, he had become one of the co-leaders of the study group, which had now tripled in size since he had started attending just four years prior. He knew his major in business administration had been the right direction for him, and he was settled on going into the job market seeking a position in that field. In the back of his mind, though, Nate sensed he was being drawn toward vocational ministry of some sort.

Within a year after graduation, Nate took a marketing position with a large national firm and married Jan, his college sweetheart. Conveniently, his company had an office just half an hour from where he grew up. He was able to maintain his roots and stay in close touch with parents and childhood friends.

Nate's career soon took off. His marketing position fit his "big idea" mentality well. He was able to garner the respect of older co-workers. Within two years, he was promoted to a supervisory role, even leading some of those older co-workers. He was placed in a fast track management program designed to groom potential leaders for more lucrative middle and senior management level positions. The future was bright.

About seven years into his career, Nate began once again to sense that same pull toward vocational ministry that he had felt his senior year of college. He and Jan had become heavily involved as volunteer leaders in an influential church located in their town. They both found that their volunteer involvement did not satisfy the itch to do ministry. Their involvement only caused the itch to grow. Discontent in being able to contribute only three to four hours a week as volunteers, they ultimately realized they were dealing with a spiritual call to become involved on a full-time basis.

Old Calling: New Career

Nate's resignation from his company surprised few who really knew him. Many gave him congratulatory statements. His passion for teenagers had become obvious. All he wanted to talk about were the kids being touched through the ministry of his church. Nate impressed his colleagues and subordinates with his handling of the significant demands of his marketing position, while spending so much volunteer time in ministry. To top things off, two young children had joined Nate and Jan's household.

With all this going on, the couple was fired up about the challenges ahead as Nate moved into their church's newly created position of Pastor of Students and Evangelism. With his reputation as a big dreamer well-established, the personnel committee asked Nate to spend roughly 20–30 percent of his time leading the church's evangelism initiative, with a focus on reaching the community through significant events. He would be free to spend the rest of his time working in his area of passion—with the rapidly developing group of teenagers forming what would become known as Living Truth Youth Ministry.

Leveraging Strengths

As the newest staff pastor at his church, Nate was able to get a lot done early on. The relationships he had built as a volunteer would prove to be very valuable. It did not hurt that the teens in the ministry already knew him, and for the most part loved him. He was in a good position, having already earned enough credibility to move things ahead. It was, all in all, a smooth transition.

Nate's corporate career had helped him develop an expertise at developing new positions that would support new initiatives. He was really strong at taking an area of need, seeing opportunities, and then putting structure around it. This resulted more than once in Nate's being asked to develop a new position to serve a new product or market. He had even gotten to the point at which he would seek out these new positions. He knew that while staffing such positions carried a potentially high risk of failure, the lack of structure in these jobs would allow him the opportunity for the autonomy he so needed. He enjoyed that autonomy, and he certainly didn't mind those inherent risks.

This corporate experience served Nate well in his new ministry position. His church had a long history of fairly strong leadership, and that leadership had developed solid infrastructural systems over the years. The church's legacy revolved around its origin as a church started to serve the burgeoning aircraft industry that had taken hold in this relatively small town. The church's personnel policies, developed many years before, even seemed to be built around the manufacturing personnel policies in those aircraft factories. In many respects, the church's operations resembled the local factories a bit too much. For the most part, however, this identity helped to facilitate the development of some fairly healthy internal systems.

■   **Nate knew that while staffing such positions carried a potentially high risk of failure, the lack of structure in these jobs would allow him opportunity for the autonomy he so needed.**

Nate quickly got a handle on these preexisting operational systems and made some significant improvements in those systems. Other than a little defensiveness from the office staff, Nate experienced little resistance from anyone. Nate gained the ear of the pastor because of the pastor's respect for Nate's abilities—abilities that the pastor realized that he himself did not possess.

By utilizing the church's existing operational systems, Nate was able to add and enhance a number of elements for the ministry.

Within the first year, he developed a security/identification system that would ultimately serve the children's ministry as well. He also developed creative fund-raising avenues and a system for holding volunteer leaders accountable for their performance. Nate's idea was that if he could put in place the proper infrastructure in the early days of the ministry, he could focus on developing his *big dreams* over the next few years.

Nate would ultimately enjoy significant success in his church and as a leader among other local and regional student ministers. The student ministry program at his church was quickly being seen as a model for other churches' ministries. Nate was having a great time, and he thought he could stay in his position forever and love it.

The Need For a Challenge

After a few years in his new position, however, Nate began to realize that he had conquered many of the big challenges. Nate was not a *maintenance man*. He had a hard time settling for working on only the day-to-day operations of an organization. He could do some minor things to make the student ministry incrementally better, but these things would not have the big positive impact he so enjoyed seeing. He thought about trying to exert greater influence at a church-wide level and to help the church develop some new and more effective systems. But his efforts had been squashed. He learned that an organization that had not developed a culture of continuous transition, even with some well-developed infrastructural systems, can lead to the organization placing artificial constraints on its employees. In Nate's case, he was the student pastor, a position which had fallen in line in the staff hierarchy below the senior pastor, educational pastor, and music pastor. As the low man on the organizational totem pole, his opportunities in bringing real change were severely limited.

■ **An organization that has not developed a culture of continuous transition, even with some well-developed infrastructural systems, can lead to the organization placing artificial constraints on its employees.**

Nate began to come to grips with the fact that his position no longer held the challenge that it once had. He had become bored. It saddened him that he felt this way. In another way he could sense a growing restlessness in his professional life. He needed a new challenge, and not just a small one.

Big Challenge—Big Change

Nate had begun studying some of the current thoughts from leaders and practitioners in the church growth movement. Seeking initially just to come away with some ideas that he could implement in his student ministry, he became intrigued with what he was seeing happen in significant churches that had taken more innovative approaches to ministry. He became attracted to a characteristic he saw in nearly all these churches—the freedom the leadership had to explore new horizons of ministry. From his studies, he concluded that the big challenges in these churches never stopped coming, simply because the innovative nature of the churches themselves served to encourage and allow leadership to grow the church through pursuit of new opportunities.

> ■ **Nate became attracted to a characteristic that he saw in nearly all these churches—the freedom the leadership had to explore new horizons of ministry.**

The more Nate read, the more he liked what he read. Nate had never been one to sense that God would send a sign to let him know about His will. Rather, in Nate's experience, God would mainly use circumstances and Nate's sense of motivation to nudge him forward. So, sensing that God might be nudging him once again, Nate decided to take inventory of his situation, to try determining whether God might be leading him in a different direction. His conclusions....

- Nate was a guy who loved big challenges. He would be bored without them.
- The student pastor position had been rich with challenge at one time, but no longer was.
- Looking at the innovative churches had exposed him to some new stuff and attracted him to these churches.
- His interest in his current position was waning more each and every day.
- Nate decided that he and Jan really needed to spend some time figuring out what God was saying to them.

Idea Incubation

Over the next three months, Nate really hit the books hard. Not his textbooks from college. Rather he set out to devour everything he could find about those churches that really seemed to *get it*. He made phone calls to pastors on the staffs of some of those churches.

He checked out Web sites that would give him more independent opinions and ideas about some of these churches. He even made a couple of weekend road trips to check out a couple of the ones that happened to be in driving distance of his home. Nate kept up his student ministry responsibilities fairly easily. After all, four years on the job, building a solid infrastructure including an experienced and dependable group of adult leaders, made him nearly able to put the ministry on auto-pilot.

By the end of the three-month period, Nate and Jan were sensing pretty clearly that their next move would be to one of these churches. Having reached this conclusion, they set out to figure out how to go about getting into one of them. Nate discovered that movement into the more innovative church staffs would not be simple. First of all, he discovered that most of these churches filled their positions through internal hirings of folks already in the church. They placed a greater emphasis on understanding the church's culture and on "on the job" track record than on formal religious-based education. Second, he discovered that the majority of these innovative churches were new church starts and that financial resources were relatively scarce. Many of these new churches saw themselves as new businesses and understood the value of reinvesting their income in the early years back into the church. Third, there simply wasn't very much turnover, and thus few employment opportunities, in these churches.

Nate began sensing that perhaps the best way for him to get into an innovative church would be to start one. After all, he considered himself an entrepreneur. He could think of no other project that would bring as great a challenge as starting a church. He thought he should move ahead. So he did!

Planning Ahead

Once Nate had settled on his decision about starting a church, he went to work—hard! He absorbed everything he could. He had decided that the best place for him to start a church was right there in the town in which he had been living since college graduation. He planned to find a meeting place on the other side of town from the church he had been serving for the past few years.

He went "underground" and shared his ideas with friends, enabling him to pull together a start team of twelve adults. Always the big dreamer, he had some big ideas about what could happen in his little town. He and the start team decided to call the church *Journey*. He knew of no other churches in town doing the things he visualized for *Journey*. He thought that would give him an advantage in branding his church.

Finally, Nate advised his pastor about his plans. The senior pastor was very supportive, as was the rest of the church. The church allowed Nate to continue working at the church and to spend as much time as necessary preparing for the church launch. Knowing that income would be a big concern, Nate gladly took the church up on its offer.

His church's positive response to his plans thrilled Nate. This shot of momentum encouraged him, Jan, and the team as they would spend many hours together planning for the launch of *Journey*. Nate felt like he was back in his old company, planning for a new product to come to market. He was really seeing how his corporate experience helped prepare him for what he would be doing. He knew he would need to get some level of credible seminary training. But he thought he could do that later on—after things at his church settled down a bit.

Big Start—Lots of Work

The launch date came, and things went well. By the end of the first month, *Journey* had nearly a hundred regular attenders. Many were from other churches, but at least half of them were a part of Journey's target group—unchurched families with children.

Nate discovered the transition from student pastor in a well-established church to lead pastor in a new church start was hardly smooth. He absolutely loved what he was doing. But he had no idea what this new world would be like until after the church actually got off the ground.

Now that they were "live," Nate's life had changed drastically. His focus now became the *"little things"*—as he liked to call them. His start team had been very helpful in the pre-launch stages and were still being very productive—particularly on Sunday mornings, filling in ministry roles and handling logistical roles—but their availability during the week was severely limited. Each of them held down a full-time position. The start team matched the targeted demographic of *Journey*. Ten of them comprised relatively young adult couples with at least two young children. One was a single guy who had a good job, but was literally on the road traveling four to five days a week. The other was a single mom with two preschool-age kids. The start team members were great. But with all their family and work obligations, they were not able to do a whole lot during the week.

Even Jan, whose excitement level had not waned, was not able to help during the week. The compensation from her position at a local CPA firm was the only steady income they had. As with the other couples, her job requirements, coupled with taking care of their young kids after a full day in day care, left her little if any time to help Nate in the day-to-day work of the new church.

■ **Nate found himself in the trenches, reviewing and inputting guest information cards, following up with phone calls, and putting together a weekly e-mail communication and the Sunday morning bulletin.**

So Nate found himself in the trenches, handling things like reviewing and inputting guest information cards into their church management software system, following up with phone calls (which he enjoyed) to nearly everyone who attended, and putting together a weekly e-mail communication as well as the Sunday morning bulletin, just to name a few tasks. He also had to spend lots of time completing state and federal government applications for nonprofit status. Also denominational paperwork requirements came with the funding awarded *Journey*.

None of these activities were overwhelming in themselves. However, Nate discovered one person administering the work of the whole church could be particularly consuming. Still riding the excitement of the successful start of *Journey*, he loved every minute of it—even those "little things" that collectively took up so much time.

Fast Forward

Twenty-four months into the start of *Journey*, things were still going well—on the surface. Weekly attendance was at about 150. The church had doubled in size since the "leveling off" after their initial launch. But the composition of those people had changed. Few of the regular attenders in the first four to five months were there anymore. Instead, they were replaced by new faces. Nate wasn't necessarily discouraged with this—he knew that some of this would be natural in a new church. Even three of his start team families had left the church. When he spoke with them, each had said, in different words, that they just weren't excited about the church like they had been just before and after the launch. Two of the couples said that their workloads on Sunday mornings kept their families from enjoying the experiences like they felt they should. They said they were no longer energized and no longer understood the real purpose behind what they were doing. Two of the couples left to go back to the church they had left before joining the *Journey* start team. The other said they were going to take a break from institutional church for a while.

While the revolving door of the church-at-large was one thing, the departure of the three start team families rocked Nate's world. He began to wonder about his own role. What had he done wrong? He had not spent a lot of time with the start team members. After all, they were a part of this from the beginning. The stakes were high, and he had figured they were all in it for the long haul, just like he was.

Harsh Reality Hits

Nate thought and thought about what had happened. He beat himself up, lamenting the fact that some of the folks who went to war with him had left his side. They were good people. They had done it the right way—by coming straight to him. They left on good terms and would likely still be friends, although things could be awkward for a while. Still, the questions came: "What could I have done differently?" "Why wasn't their level of commitment high enough to stick it out?" "Where do I go from here?"

Out of the conversations with the departing start team couples, one particular item seemed to haunt Nate: they said *they were no longer energized.* After thinking about this long and hard, he had to admit that he hardly ever talked about the things he used to talk about in the pre-launch days, or even in the first five or six months of the church. He realized that he had begun to assume that the start team, and even many who came to the church after launch, *got it.* He figured that they surely understood what they were doing and why.

Yet apparently they didn't.

> ■ Nate had to admit that he hardly ever talked about the things he used to talk about in the pre-launch days, or even in the first five or six months of the church. He realized that he had begun to assume that the start team, and even many who came to the church after launch, "got it."

What had really happened?

Nate had maintained close friendships with a couple of his former corporate buddies, Jay and Brad. Both had climbed the corporate ladder along with Nate, and both had attained mid-level executive positions in the company. Nate had talked to them fairly regularly over the years since he had entered vocational ministry—always on more of a social basis. They had even done a few things together as families over the years. Now Nate wanted to get with these guys, going even beyond their friendships for some professional advice. Nate needed a sounding board, and who better than his old buddies—pretty sharp guys in their own right! Even though neither of them claimed to be committed men of faith, he respected them and wanted to get their perspective on what may be going wrong.

A Leadership Summit

Nate's buddies were pretty quick to respond to Nate's desire to get together. The week after he called, the three found themselves one evening at one of their favorite restaurants from their old corporate days. After exchanging some corporate war stories that had grown in extravagance over the years, Nate got into the past couple of years of his life with *Journey*. For nearly an hour the guys listened as Nate poured out his story. In many ways, Nate felt that he had never fully articulated such an honest combination of the facts, and his feelings about those facts. As Nate laid out his story, some things began to come to mind that he hadn't thought about before. He felt like he was getting a little more clarity on the situation just by talking through it.

Finishing his story, he looked at the guys and asked, "What do you think?" Jay was the first to speak, "You surely have been in the trenches these past two years. You never had to address envelopes for mass mailing at the company…"

That statement said a lot to Nate. Brad picked up on Jay's line of thinking, "Sounds like you're doing lots of the types of things we did in those first few months with the company, when they were testing our willingness to do anything! There were days I felt like I was so involved in nitty-gritty details that I thought I would never be able to see beyond my cubicle! For you, it's like déjà vu all over again! I couldn't do what you've been doing!"

This line of conversation continued for another twenty minutes. Nate felt as if revelation after revelation was coming to him as he heard the guys' statements and his responses. Finally he grabbed a napkin and started scribbling his thoughts…

Been bogged down in details too much…
Tried to do too much myself—not enough delegation…
Focus on detail—lost focus on big picture…

Have felt guilty asking start team to do stuff. They're not getting
  paid for it… I am… After all, the church is "my project."
Am I a control freak, in wanting to do so much of it myself?
How do I get out of this mode of operation?

A full hour and a half later, Nate felt as if the weight of the world
had been lifted off his shoulders. He knew the problem hadn't gone
away, but he did feel now that he had an idea of what the problem
actually was. When he got home that night, he decided to do a
little more writing. Finally, after Jan got up and gently chastised
him about needing his rest, he tried to write one statement that
summarized what he had discovered that evening:

> I've lost my sense of vision. Before the church got started, I
> had lots of vision! I even thought I had a particular vision for
> *Journey*. But once the church started, the real work began. As
> soon as the first Sunday came, I realized I was really a lead
> pastor now. I had to do everything—or at least I thought I
> had to do everything. Two factors contributed to this:
>
> • This is the project God gave to ME! So I am responsible
>   for it. I hesitate to ask others to do stuff—because
>   God gave it to me!
> • I want it done right. Professionally, this is by far the
>   biggest thing I've ever done. I know how I want it
>   done, and too often I've done it myself instead of
>   involving others.

Even though Nate spent his evening focusing on problems—
real problems, he went to bed and slept better than he had in quite
a while.

Clarity on the Real Issue

Nate began to realize that evening that he had fallen into a
trap—one that many entrepreneurs fall into, whether they start
a business, a church, or some other type of organization. Most
organizations are started by legitimate visionary thinkers. Many
of them may in fact be at their best in the months and weeks prior
to the start of the organization. That is when their dreams are the
most alive. Their creative juices flow as they think about what could
happen. True entrepreneurs often have the ability to dream—they
are effective visionaries, but *they also have the ability to operate in
other dimensions as well.* The difference between a visionary and

an entrepreneur is that the entrepreneur will have some ability to move the vision forward by operating effectively in at least one of the others—missional, strategic, and/or tactical.

■ **The entrepreneur's ability to get things started often causes him or her to get involved too deeply in the details in attempting to make things work.**

That entrepreneurs can usually function in multiple dimensions is perhaps their greatest attribute and perhaps their greatest curse. That ability to dream, and then move on that dream, is what often get things started. On the other hand, *that ability to get things started often causes them to get involved too deeply in the details in attempting to make things work.* The result often is that the entrepreneur, whose sense of vision is so important in getting the organization started, ultimately gets heavily involved in the day-to-day operations of the organization. As the focus shifts from vision, which is critically important, to operations, which is also critically important, the tendency of the leader/entrepreneur is often to stay there in operations. After all, now that the dream has been dreamt and the vision driven the organization's start-up, things have to be done to make it all work!

■ **The real question is whether the leader/entrepreneur can know when to toggle back and forth between visionary thinking and leadership and the need to be involved in the tactical dimension.**

Ownership is never a question for the true entrepreneur, whether starting a business or a church. It's only natural that the one with the heart for getting the organization going jumps right in to help make it all happen. However, the cost to the organization for this may be great. The real question is whether the leader/entrepreneur can know when to toggle back and forth between visionary thinking and leadership and the need to be involved in the tactical dimension. If the leader gets stuck in the tactical, or even strategic, dimension, then the organization is in danger of losing the visionary leadership that it so desperately needs—particularly in the formative stages of the organization's life.

Driving Forces

Often two key factors cause entrepreneurial leaders to get too deeply involved in details: *Guilt* and *Control*.

The Guilt Complex

Marcus Buckingham speaks about one of the thirty-five areas of strength identifiable in people. He defines the strength of *responsibility*:

> Your Responsibility theme forces you to take psychological ownership for anything you commit to, and whether large or small, you feel emotionally bound to follow it through to completion. Your good name depends on it. If for some reason you cannot deliver, you automatically start to look for ways to make it up to the other person... This conscientiousness, this near obsession for doing things right, and your impeccable ethics, combine to create your reputation: utterly dependable. When assigning new responsibilities, people will look to you first because they know it will get done.[1]

Many entrepreneurs have this great sense of responsibility. It contributes to their getting something new going, and it motivates them to stay with it to make things work. Often the strength of responsibility can become a near obsession. When that happens, *a sense of responsibility can turn to a sense of guilt*.

This sense of guilt may arise because the entrepreneur, sensing his or her own responsibility, becomes hesitant to ask others to do things for the organization, even though they may be ready and willing to do whatever necessary. The attitude may be something like this: "*It's my job, I've got to do it! I can't ask someone else.*" Getting it done without having to trouble someone else is like a badge of honor. The idea is, "If I ask someone to do something, I may be imposing on them, and I don't want to do that!"

This can become a dangerous cycle because the more task-oriented that the entrepreneurial leader becomes, the less he or she will focus on the big picture for the organization. Ultimately the organization could lose its edge in the market.

■ **This sense of guilt may arise because the entrepreneur, sensing his or her own responsibility, becomes hesitant to ask others to do things for the organization, even though they may be ready and willing to do whatever necessary.**

---

[1] Marcus Buckingham and Donald O. Clifton, *Now Discover Your Strengths* (New York: The Free Press, 2001), 111.

The Control Freak

The other key factor is the issue of control. This, too, can grow out of a near obsession with responsibility. However, the idea here is less about the fear of imposing on others by asking them to perform operational tasks. It is more about the attitude that says, "I must do it myself because nobody else can do it the right way." This results in a reluctance to let others in. The short-term result can be frustration for those who don't get involved. In the long-term, the organization whose leadership doesn't let go of responsibilities will find it more difficult to drive ownership among its people. Usually, if this situation persists, *micromanagement becomes the practice of leadership, and a culture of bureaucracy emerges*. This leads ultimately to an inability of the organization to attract the best people—those who want to be challenged in their work.

> **The control freak says, "I must do it myself because nobody else can do it the right way."**

Churches and church leaders are certainly just as susceptible as their corporate counterparts to leadership affected by guilt and control issues. As a matter of fact, this is precisely what happened with Nate and his church. The natural visionary, who had always been a dreamer, started a new organization out of that sense of vision. His sense of responsibility made him overly reluctant to ask others to work hard, as he didn't want to impose too much on them. A part of him was reluctant to release responsibilities to others. He was used to striving for excellence from his corporate days and wanted to make sure that would be the hallmark of *Journey*. He simply didn't trust others to deliver that excellence like he could!

Escaping the Trap

How can a visionary leader ensure that getting involved in the details has a minimal impact on the sense of vision? Entrepreneurial leaders' sense of ownership will always lead them, to some degree, into the realm of the tactical. How can they live in two worlds—the visionary world as well as the tactical world? Here are a few thoughts.

- *Understand the inevitability of the trap.* Be aware the trap is there. The typical entrepreneurial leader, as much as he or she would probably like to have hands in all the operations— usually to make sure things are done right—will need to remember that he or she can't do everything. (This realization can be a stunning blow to the entrepreneur.) The leader, like everyone else in the organization, must focus in areas of personal strength.

- *Maintain a long-term perspective.* The entrepreneurial leader has to remain aware at all times that, as much as his or her expertise may be needed at the tactical level, others in the organization will be performing those functions on a regular basis in the future. He or she must remember that over the long haul of the organization, his or her visionary capabilities are much more important to the organization than his or her hands-on abilities. The sense of vision must be kept clear for the organization to achieve long-term health and success.
- *Get the right people on board early in the process.* Whether in a new organizational start-up or beginning a significant transition in the organization, the leader would do well to bring together a team with varied skill sets and perspectives.

■ **The entrepreneur's visionary capabilities are much more important to the organization than his or her hands-on abilities.**

- *Listen to other visionary thinkers in the organization.* Their ideas may inform and enhance the leader's vision.
- *Gather some "big project people"* to help develop the organization's missional initiatives and to help monitor and measure progress toward accomplishing those initiatives. The leader will bring along some high-powered problem solvers to develop the strategic thrusts that will break through the obstacles facing the organization.
- *Highly motivated and dependable people are needed* to make sure that missional and strategic plans are effectively executed.
- *Make "working yourself out of a job (WYOJ)" a core organizational value.* WYOJ by far works best in organizations that are led by strong visionaries, and that are naturally aggressive in seeking out new opportunities. The idea here is that employees/members are constantly mentoring and training others to ultimately bring them along to do their jobs. Driving this type of culture can be a difficult initiative for an organization, simply because of the inherent insecurities that so many people have. For example, a typical response may sound something like this: "If I work myself out of a job, and help someone else take it over, then I may not have a job." The truth is that those who work themselves out of a job will likely be those really good employees or volunteers who will have more job security than

anyone else, simply because they are likely the ones who will take on new challenges. WYOJ organizations usually attract very good people, as they will enjoy the challenges such a culture will bring. Also, turnover is low and organizational morale is high in these organizations.

■   **In a WYOJ organization, employees/members are constantly mentoring and training others in an effort to ultimately bring them along to do their jobs.**

Pulling It Together

Entrepreneurial leaders are often characterized by having a great sense of vision. This will lead them to start new ventures and to take on tough turnaround projects. However, at some point the entrepreneur's inevitable movement into the missional, strategic, and even tactical, levels of the organization's planning and execution could lead to an impairment of that vision. For example, an entrepreneurial pastor starts a new congregation and has a pretty clear idea of how things should be done in the new congregation. Justifiably so, the pastor gets involved in the strategic and tactical dimensions. In the short-term, this is probably healthy for the congregation. Often the leader *gets stuck* working in one of these dimensions and has a difficult time getting back to his or her visionary perspective. The leader's visionary focus, so critical in starting the congregation, can get lost. The congregation can get bogged down, and, over time, forward movement may stall.

Because the entrepreneurial leader's sense of vision is so critically important to the long-term health of the organization, the entrepreneurial leader must avoid this trap. The leader can maintain focus on the vision, primarily by maintaining an awareness that this potential trap exists and by developing complementary people to take on missional, strategic, and tactical roles and responsibilities. Furthermore, the leader must overcome any personal insecurity to be able to release responsibility and authority to other capable organizational members.

12

The Dimensions of Planning in the Nonreligious Organization

The *4D* planning process is transferable to any organizational setting. It will work in the congregation, and it will work in a nonreligious organization. This book has focused primarily on the use of the Four Dimensions of Planning in the congregation. Certainly, this planning process can work very well in that context. When applied properly, it can have major impact on the health of the church. *An organization is an organization,* however. The principles that drive health will work across different organizational types. Even the application of those principles will be very similar.

Religious and Nonreligious Organizations: Lots in Common!

I get so tired of hearing church folks make statements like, "That may work in the business world, but it won't work in the church!" More appropriate may be the question, "If it works in business, why can't it work in the church?" Organizations that desire to be healthy will do many of the same things. Important similarities should unite churches and businesses in their planning processes.

Each Serves Customers

Organizations have customers. Organizations will develop around a need, or a perceived need, among a group of people. Entrepreneurs generally are those who see that need and are motivated to do something to address that need. Organizations exist for a variety of reasons. Typically, they are started because of opportunities for monetary profit or because of altruistic motives.

For a business to be effective in the long run, it must get to know its customers, understand their needs, and determine how to meet those needs in an economical fashion. The business must then learn to do this on a consistent basis, with a willingness and ability to reinvent itself so that it can remain relevant over time. To be viable, it must always look for ways to increase its market share.

■ **To be effective in the long run, any organization must get to know its customers, understand their needs, and determine how to meet those needs in an economical fashion.**

A church is no different. According to the Great Commission in Matthew 28, the church's primary motive should be to *create an environment that is conducive to life change among its people.*

> "Therefore, go and make disciples of all the nations, baptizing them in the name of the Father and the Son and the Holy Spirit. Teach these new disciples to obey all the commands I have given you. And be sure of this: I am with you always, even to the end of the age." (Mt. 28:19–20)

To develop that environment for life change, an individual church must understand the people that it exists to serve. The church must discover the things it does well and how those things can best serve its people. It must focus on those things consistently, over time, always seeking to improve, finding new ways to do things more economically. The healthy church will never be satisfied with status quo, but will always look to increase its market share—the size of the church family—by attracting those who are not already in church. As a result, the church creates a climate of long-term viability.

■ **The healthy church will never be satisfied with status quo, but will always look to increase its market share—the size of the church family—by attracting those who are not already in church.**

Each Delivers a Bottom Line

Whether an organization is driven by a profit motive or by a more altruistic motive, it must have a bottom line that measures its degree of success. In a for-profit business, the bottom line will include measures of profitability, such as net income, earnings per share of stock, dividend pay out to shareholders, etc. Those measures may not be as clear and quantifiable in a church, but a church's bottom line is certainly measurable. The measure must flow out of an understanding of what it does. As we said above, the Great Commission gives all churches the mandate to create an environment that is conducive to life change among its people. That being the case, the church must adopt a measurement system that tracks this life change. A church then must define in its own context what that continuum of change looks like and how to determine when a step on that continuum has occurred.

■   **The church must adopt a measurement system that tracks life change.**

A great example of a church's understanding of its bottom line and how it can be tracked comes from Saddleback Church. Pastor Rick Warren describes the *Circles of Commitment* used to measure progress in terms of life change. The Saddleback illustration depicts those outside the church in the outer circle and those with the highest commitment level at the innermost circle.[1] While the Saddleback model itself may not fit all churches, it gives at least a good starting point for the development of a tracking system that can measure the degree of life change in those the church is called to serve. As a side note, a number of quality software packages are designed to help churches in this tracking process.

The Five Circles of Commitment

Community

Crowd

Congregation

Committed

Core

---

[1]Rick Warren, *The Purpose Driven Church* (Grand Rapids: Zondervan, 1995), 131–34.

Each Seeks to Be Innovative

To have long-term viability, any organization—for-profit or nonprofit—must be innovative in its approach. The church must keep abreast of shifts in its own internal context, as well as in its environmental context, and must be positioned to move proactively to address those shifts. It must change its own ways to meet the changing spiritual, emotional, relational, and even physical needs of those that it serves. This refers to what we described earlier as a *culture of continuous transition.*

> ■ Innovative businesses and churches will seek to develop new methods, products, services, etc., with great intentionality, and not just for the sake of simply "doing new things."

Likewise, a healthy business that seeks greater profitability will constantly try to develop new ways to meet the demand of its market. Competition in the business world is likely to be fierce, and a healthy company must keep one eye on its current operations and the other on its future. *The innovative business, like the innovative church, will seek to develop new methods, products, services, etc., with great intentionality, not just for the sake of "doing new things."* It will not be afraid to try new things. It will not fear failure but *will see a failed attempt as a step on the road toward eventual success.*

Each Should Strive for Excellence

An organization should never come into existence unless it has a stated goal of *commitment to excellence* in all it does. Excellence must permeate the organization—from the way it hires and handles its employees, to the way it develops its internal processes and delivers products and services, to the way it interfaces with its customers. To do otherwise would be a waste of resources—human and financial resources.

As with innovation, churches that strive for excellence will be those most likely to create environments in which life change can occur. In business, a consistent quest for excellence will constitute a significant competitive advantage for the business itself.

Each Gives Paychecks

One of the major organizational paradoxes I have seen, having experienced leading in a corporate business environment and in a church environment, is the difference between leading those employees who are motivated—at least partially—by a monetary paycheck and those volunteers in a church who are motivated by

_____ (you fill in the blank). I must admit that the way I state this paradox seems to assume that everyone's primary motivation is money. Certainly this is not the case. Looking at paycheck motivation does raise an interesting question: "Is it more difficult to lead in the volunteer church world than in the corporate world? After all, isn't money—the payoff for a job well done in a business—a greater motivator?" Even though I have worked extensively in both worlds, I still don't think I know the answer to that question.

One of the most valuable lessons I have learned in leading a church is that *we can still give paychecks to those volunteers*. In our American culture, we have come to relate so much to money. *"Follow the money..."* is perhaps one of the most overworked, but relevant, phrases in television and movies. This phrase is certainly not limited to entertainment forums. We tend to forget, however, that people need to feel good about themselves, about their accomplishments—no matter where their work is played out. In the corporate world, for the vast majority of employees, drawing a paycheck is not enough. They also need positive reinforcement. Numerous workplace studies over the years have shown this, again and again, to be true.

■   **The church, while it cannot give monetary paychecks to everyone who contributes, can, and must, learn how to give paychecks of encouragement and recognition.**

Likewise the church, while it cannot give monetary paychecks to everyone who contributes, can, and must, learn how to give paychecks of encouragement and recognition. The church must be consistent in conveying to its people the value of their contributions. These paychecks don't always have to be in the form of public recognition. Some churches overdo the "public recognition from the platform" thing. Rather, for most people, it's the spontaneous word of appreciation or note in the mail that triggers the feeling of value on the part of the individual.

Resisting the Tyranny of the Urgent

No matter the type of organization, the 4D planning process will work nicely when applied with intentionality, consistency, and patience. One of the biggest deterrents to developing a culture of continuous transition is a tendency to give in to the *tyranny of the urgent*.

To be effective, the congregation must make a serious commitment to the planning process and be willing to follow through with the initiatives that flow from the process. As with any planning process, the temptation to revert to the urgency of the organization's day-to-day operations is strong.

Likewise, a business will face the regular temptation to succumb to the pressures of the day-to-day. A healthy company will set its short-term goals and objectives with the company's long-term health in view. In the short run, the business still must closely watch its bottom line. Maintaining this long-term/short-term perspective may make it difficult for a business to focus on the planning process.

Compared to the church, the business with a financial profit motive and with paid employees who devote a greater portion of their time to the business will normally have greater resources to allocate toward the planning process. In relation to their counterparts in a church, employees in a business may also be more likely to have a singular focus on either operations or planning, depending on their assignment. The healthy business, then, may have an even better chance of success with the 4D planning process.

Pulling It Together

The 4D planning process is transferable to any organizational setting. While most nonreligious for-profit organizations will be, by nature, more *bottom-line results-oriented* than religious organizations, *planning with intentionality* must be a high priority. For example, organizational health can be spurred on by the emphasis on engaging employees within the dimension in which they are best equipped to contribute. This will increase ownership among employees and will result in higher employee satisfaction, higher productivity, and lower turnover. As employees take more ownership, they can be more empowered as decision-making responsibilities are transitioned away from the top levels of management and closer to those who *make it happen*.

13

The Church Deserves the Best

October 13, 1992, I believe it was. I was sitting with some friends at a local pizza restaurant. In our Sunday evening tradition, we jumped into our cars and headed over to the restaurant after the evening service at our somewhat traditional church. We were a group of thirty-something couples who had forged some close friendships. In our usual routine, we husbands sat together. Our wives migrated toward the other end of the table—of course taking with them the kids, who were sitting in their laps, high chairs, or booster seats. Waiting for our food, we were joking, laughing, and relishing the moments on the eve of the beginning of another work week.

Unexpectedly, moments of relative silence enveloped us. You know those moments—the laughter had died down after a funny line from one of the table's occupants. We were all waiting for someone else to come up with another funny line. The youth pastor, who also doubled as one of my good friends, seemed to make it a point that night to sit by me. Just as the anticipated next funny line came, and folks around the table burst out laughing, my youth pastor / friend turned to me, almost directly in my ear, and began talking under his breath. I felt a little weird at first. I had a hard time hearing him and had to ask him a couple of times to repeat his question.

After the second repetition, I made out what he asked me: "*Are you ready to take over?*"

Even after I understood the words he spoke, I sill had no idea what he was talking about. So I asked him what he meant.

He told me in a pretty straightforward—though still hushed—manner: *"I'm leaving this church to move into another position at a different church. God's made that clear to me. And He's made it pretty clear that you're the guy to take over my job now."*

For a brief moment I considered his words and informed him of my conclusion: I *laughed in his face*—which, by the way, was still pretty close to my face. Anyway, after I laughed, I felt badly, realizing that he had confided in me information that probably no one else—outside his family—had been privy to. Therefore, I knew I had to go into the "hush" mode as I talked to him a little further about this. After he assured me that he was as serious as he could be, I looked him in the eye and said, "Gary, *you know what I make, and I know what YOU make! There is no way!"*

I have to admit that I had really enjoyed my corporate life! I had been there nearly ten years with a great company and had worked hard. The company had treated me well and had given me great opportunities for growth. I had realized for some time that I simply had received God's favor in my career. I certainly didn't deserve it. After all, I'm not that smart. But somehow it worked. I had been promoted a few times and was regularly encouraged to move to new positions that would further challenge me. I really liked it. But I have to admit, in my mind, I had been asking questions such as, *"Is there really something more out there? Is there something else that would be even more challenging for me?"* But—becoming a youth pastor?! I mean—this was the "low man on the totem pole" position in traditional churches (no offense intended). Gary wanted me to move from being a mid-level corporate executive to the position in the church just above the part-time maintenance man.

As I sat there that evening at the restaurant, I felt sure that I wouldn't give Gary's words a second thought. But how was I to know that as I dressed for work the next morning, those words would come back over and over again. Somehow, some way, this idea had a weird sort of appeal. I couldn't put my finger on it.

Anyway, much to Gary's delight, I found myself in the pastor's office just a couple of weeks later. I told him of the conversation between Gary and me, and how I sensed the Holy Spirit drawing me toward the position and thus toward a significant career change. His response really blew me away. Just as I had laughed in Gary's face a couple of weeks earlier at the restaurant, my pastor laughed in mine! He said something like, *"I think I know about what you make in your job, and I know what Gary makes in his. There's no way!"*

A Risk Worth Taking

That meeting, believe it or not, began to solidify things in my mind. Despite the pastor's disbelief that I would consider such a move, I could sense even more after the meeting that it was the direction I was to take. After all, *what better thing to do with my life than to devote it to the furthering of the movement that God had started, with the intent of turning the world to Himself.*

The next couple of months brought the challenge of dealing with the church hiring process while at the same time trying to keep my candidacy a secret. After all, a number of people in our church worked for our company, and I knew that if word of my candidacy with the church got out to my vice-president, I would have lots of explaining to do.

About four months after that fateful night at the pizza restaurant, I assumed the youth pastor position at our church. After starting at the church, I went to the pastor and asked him why, in our earlier meeting, he had been no more excited about the idea of me taking the position. I'll never forget what he told me: *"It's not that I didn't want you to take the position. It's just that I really liked the big Christmas gift you give me each year, and I knew if you took the youth pastor position, you wouldn't be able to afford to do that anymore!"* At least he was honest—and he was right!

My four years on the staff of that strong old church did me a lot of good. Besides being a really fun part of my life, it provided a good transitional phase between my corporate life and what God would bring me to do next!

Here We Go Again!

Coming up on four years in that youth pastor position, God was now making it clear to me that the next big step was to leave the relatively comfortable staff role at this fairly sizeable traditional church, to start a new church in the same town. Changing careers— again—was going to be exciting for me. After all, I'm the kind of guy who loves new challenges! For my wife—well, that's a different story. She'd get used to it. I had just "led" her through a major step four years earlier, having left the corporate world for vocational ministry.

The four years on staff at the traditional church had brought lots of different experiences. Most were very good, but some were not so good. Whatever the experiences, they had helped to frame some real learnings, and in conjunction with my stint in the corporate world, these experiences helped prepare me for an entirely new vocational role.

The Hope of the World

"The local church is the hope of the world..." This statement by Bill Hybels did more than anything to put into words what I had always known—and really believed. Yet I don't know that I had ever thought of the church that way. I had always thought of the church as the house that Christ built, as the most important institution the world had ever known, and the most influential as well. But I don't know that I had ever seen the church's role as clearly as I now did. *"The hope of the world..."* What a huge statement—and yet God called me—little old me—to be a leader in a small piece of this movement. Wow!

Hybels explains the rationale for his conclusion about the church:

> There is nothing like the local church when it's working right. Its beauty is indescribable. Its power is breathtaking. Its potential is unlimited. It comforts the grieving and heals the broken in the context of community. It builds bridges to seekers and offers truth to the confused. It provides resources for those in need and opens its arms to the forgotten, the downtrodden, the disillusioned. It breaks the chains of addictions, frees the oppressed, and offers hope to the marginalized in this world. Whatever the capacity for human suffering, the church has a greater capacity for healing and wholeness.[1]

There's more to what Hybels said. Here is the complete original quote: *"The local church is the hope of the world and its future rests primarily in the hands of its leaders."*

Not only is the church the hope of the world, but, if Hybels is right, then God has taken the steering wheel for the church—that His Son Jesus Christ died for—and He has placed it in the collective hands of the leaders He has ordained for the church. Now that is humbling—and a little scary.

So—God created the world, and all of us who are a part of it. He intended for us to live in perfect harmony with Him, but sin crept into humanity from the temptation of the first man and woman

---

[1]Bill Hybels, *Courageous Leadership* (Grand Rapids: Zondervan, 2002), 23.

by Satan, the evil deceiver. God's plan for redemption included sending to earth His only Son as a Redeemer, as the perfect sacrifice for our sins. His ultimate death and miraculous resurrection would provide both the means for, and the proof of, that redemption. When the job was done, He would return to His father. But before His return, he would plant the seed for something big, something that would be incredibly powerful—the birth and subsequent growth of the church—the hope of the world. Before His death, Jesus would say of the church in Matthew 16:18, "I will build my church, and all the powers of hell will not conquer it."

It surely sounds like a really big deal, and indeed it has been, and will continue to be. "The church is truly the hope of the world and its future rests primarily in the hands of its leaders."

Best Practices

Since the church is God's institution designed for changing the world and turning it to Himself, and since its leaders have a special delegation from God for directing the church with the guidance of the Holy Spirit, is there any reason to justify giving the church less than the best we have to offer? Of course not! That was the conclusion I had come to when faced with the decision of whether to follow God's leading for me to take the youth pastor position, and then again four years later to start Integrity Church. Once I decided to take on the challenge, I decided that I had no choice but to commit to lead in the church with the best "lifestyle leadership" and "leadership tools" available.

Since a lot of what happens positively in an organization comes out of good, solid planning, perhaps that is the first area in our churches that needs to be shored up! After all, God honors planning. His Word is pretty clear on that. He reserves the right, however, to change our plans and the course of our direction whenever He wants. Proverbs 16:9 says, "We can make our plans, but the Lord determines our steps." Because God honors planning, we must do the best job we can in planning—particularly for the church!

Best Planning

The *4D* planning paradigm provides an organization with a systematic approach to a relatively difficult process. Done well, the Four Dimensions process provides a flexible template for tailoring organizational planning to the uniqueness of the organization. In doing this, it produces a number of benefits:

- Identification and deployment of organizational members in terms of their planning perspectives, i.e., visionary, missional, strategic, and tactical.
- Ownership that comes with engaging members with the opportunity to have relevant and significant input into the planning process.
- Opportunity for developing a culture of continuous transition and thus continuous improvement.
- Opportunity for greater alignment between the vision of the organization and the actual day-to-day operations of the organization.

■   **Is there any reason to justify giving the church less than the best we have to offer? Of course not!**

The *4D* planning process, then, is a tool that helps the organization identify and implement the very best it has to offer. When organizations are able to give the very best they have to offer, everybody wins.

For the innovative business organization, it means maximizing its market share, profitability, and hopefully its positive effects on the community.

For the innovative congregation, it means maximizing its impact on the Kingdom of God and fulfilling the unique plan that God has established for it. It's all about the church being "...*the hope of the world.*"

About the Author

Bud Wrenn is the founding pastor of Integrity Church (www. integritycommunity.org), a growing Purpose-Driven congregation in Burlington, North Carolina, and the founding director of the Innovative Church Community (www.innovativechurches.org), an organization committed to providing leadership development opportunities for leaders of non-profit organizations. He is the Founder & President of Pinnacle Consulting & Coaching Group (www.pinnacleccg.org), and is a consulting partner with The Table Group, the consulting firm of Patrick Lencioni, Table Group president and the author of the book *The Five Dysfunctions of a Team*.

During Bud's ten-year career with AT&T, he held various supervisory and mid-level management positions. Bud and wife, Tammy, have three children.

For additional resources and tools associated with *Innovative Planning: Your Church in 4-D*, go to www.innovativeplanning.org and www.pinnacleccg.org.